What people are s

To Sing with Bard

To Sing with Bards and Angels weaves together the fertile worlds of our spiritual and creative lives with the natural world and the realm of Spirit, illustrating with personal stories, poems and suggestions for practice how the relationship between these worlds is intimate, inseparable and life-enriching. Iona Jenkins' gentle wisdom illuminates the landscape of the heart and the song of the soul in each of us.
Eimear Burke, Chosen Chief of The Order of Bards, Ovates and Druids

Poet and artist Iona Jenkins has spun a luminous tapestry, interwoven with conversations with her muse and wise inner guide, the Angel Astariel. This lyrical book which moves back and forth across the borders between waking reality and the province of dreams is a joyful celebration of life lived in harmony with the Spirit that flows through all things. Through the author's eyes, we experience the sensual magic of the sacred lands from Arizona to Nepal, and Italy, then back to her home in Wales with its Druidic and Arthurian mysteries. Along the way, we discover how to connect with our souls by opening to the living world of Nature through simple exercises to align our lives with the seasons, to commune with the trees, to embrace the wisdom of the animal kingdom. This book is sure to inspire everyone who longs for a life filled with creativity and a spirituality that embraces both the outer beauty of the Earth and the inner beauty of the soul.
Mara Freeman, author of *Kindling the Celtic Spirit and Grail Alchemy*, **Director of the Avalon Mystery School**

Some see visions and express them in words, marble, paint, clay or music. But where do these visions come from? Tracing her own spiritual journey through Celtic mysteries, Buddhism, art and meditation, Iona Jenkins suggests myriad ways to call down angels of inspiration to ignite your own creative forces. *To Sing with Bards and Angels* is a fascinating original book.
Vicki Mackenzie, author of several books on Buddhism including, *Cave in the Snow, Why Buddhism?* and *The Revolutionary Life of Freda Bedi*

A beautifully crafted book full of evocative poetry and wonderful prose.
Jack Scott, author of *Perking the Pansies* and *Turkey Street*

To Sing with
Bards and Angels

A Journey into the Creative Heart

To Sing with Bards and Angels

A Journey into the Creative Heart

Iona Jenkins

HN HUNT PUBLISHIN

Winchester, UK
Washington, USA

JOHN HUNT PUBLISHING

First published by O-Books, 2022
O-Books is an imprint of John Hunt Publishing Ltd., 3 East St., Alresford,
Hampshire SO24 9EE, UK
office@jhpbooks.com
www.johnhuntpublishing.com
www.o-books.com

For distributor details and how to order please visit the 'Ordering' section on our website.

Text copyright: Iona Jenkins 2021

ISBN: 978 1 80341 074 6
978 1 80341 075 3 (ebook)
Library of Congress Control Number: 2021947887

A CIP catalogue record for this book is available from the British Library.

Design: Matthew Greenfield

UK: Printed and bound by CPI Group (UK) Ltd, Croydon, CR0 4YY
Printed in North America by CPI GPS partners

We operate a distinctive and ethical publishing philosophy in
all areas of our business, from our global network of authors to
production and worldwide distribution.

Contents

Other titles by this Author

Heartsong, 2016
ASIN: B01MSRD1BC

The Starlit Door, 2018
ASIN: B07CVLJ9CZ

Dedication

To Chalice Well in Glastonbury, always a garden of my heart, where people of all creeds and cultures may meet in peace and friendship, for the sharing of wisdom.

Introduction

To Sing with Bards and Angels is intended as a signpost towards a door of possibility, for anyone aspiring to explore a creative spiritual path.

Once upon a time in Italy, after spending a day surrounded by masterpieces of sacred art and sculpture in Rome, an idea began to take shape. I was enjoying an October break, at the home of Italian friends, in the province of Lazio, when only a short stroll from their front door, I came across a convenient bench. Soon I was sitting quietly with my notebook in the late afternoon sunshine, my senses filling with peaceful impressions from the surrounding landscape. Rising behind me, in the distance, Monte Semprevisa's peak stretched my awareness towards the sky. The scents and colors of warm earth and garden trees heavy with ripe lemons, seemed to mingle in sunlight, with my previous day's memories of sculptures and paintings, visions of beautiful, winged beings, the inspiration of so many great artists. I began to write a poem that would become a first step towards exploring creative spirituality through these pages.

I named that poem "The Language of Angels" (see chapter 2), because it seemed as though Rome's angelic art had become magically entwined with my experience of nature in that moment. The result was a blend of color, images, music, warmth, belonging, like the world's fabric had been enlivened by the sound of angels speaking or singing their words of inspiration, for my heart to translate into its own lines of poetry. In Celtic culture, the Bards or Druid storytellers and poets know this stream of inspiration as *Awen* (pronounced Ah-wen). It is a Welsh/Cornish/Breton word that translates as *Flowing Spirit*, and it sings beautifully.

A few years later, when the angels caught my attention again, the first chapter of a book emerged from a meditation prompted by moonlight, reflecting on the sea outside my window in Wales. As I contemplated the shining path created by a full moon across the still waters of Môr Hafren (Bristol Channel), an impression arose of a loving, creative Presence, that seemed to exist not only deep within the internal world of my intuitive mind, but also as an integral part of the illuminated sea and landscape outside. I saw this Presence as an angel, a reflection of the moon on water, an otherworldly being, whose spiritual and artistic wisdom could be channeled and translated from a harmonic language of symbols and light into words of descriptive, poetry and prose I enjoy writing so much.

Although the ideas I offer come from my own creative journey, they contain helpful pointers for anyone aspiring to live a spiritually creative life. I hope that each one of my readers will allow themselves the freedom to interpret these signs according to their personal spiritual background and to choose the direction their path will take before traveling at their own pace.

I have discovered ways to heal my own emotional wounds, improve my health, increase my spiritual awareness, my sense of belonging and ability to celebrate life, by writing my path into being, creating spiritual direction through my art. I have chosen, then, to work in the *Flowing Spirit*, by not only including intuitive dialogue between myself and the Angel Presence of those moonlight meditations, but also through personal tales, poetry, and reflections from my journey.

Reciting my own poems in bardic voice, I have placed one at the beginning of each chapter to guide the reader over its threshold into an adventure. I then continue my journey, painting snippets from both my internal and external spiritual travels, in words, flowing through a stream of beauty and color as I experience it. Each chapter ends with an optional task and/or meditation, but since meditation has the power to open the mind, it is advisable, especially when working with the moon, to only attempt some of these exercises if they feel right for you. In times of turbulence, it is often more appropriate to slow down, practice relaxation, stay grounded and allow life to flow gently around a peaceful shore.

I invite you to become my spiritual traveling companion through the chapters of this book, as I follow my creative spirit, across external landscapes, and the internal worlds of unconscious mind. At journey's end, perhaps you might be encouraged to explore further. The decision to present this work in descriptive bardic voice and creative form, is intended to demonstrate *Flowing Spirit* in action. I have also tried to remain as non-directive as possible, allowing you enough space and freedom to hear the angels singing your own song.

May your passion for life and the love in your heart inspire you to create.

Iona

Chapter One

A Language of Angels

Full Moon Meditation

The moon has cast a path of light
across the water straight and true
from shores of Wales to Somerset
in silvered streams of peaceful dreams
a star shines bright in deep night skies
and soft waves breaking on the shore
I hear the surging notes of Oran Mór,
the Greatest Song that sang them all.
Iona Jenkins

This full moon is going to keep me awake, so I decide to stay up for an hour or so. I light a candle lantern in the doorway, where my balcony looks out over the darkened sea. Next, I drape a blanket around my shoulders to stay warm with both door and heart open to the still night air, the lilting music from the harp of the ocean and the bliss of being able to float upon the notes of the Great Song, which in Gaelic is known as Oran Mór. These words expressing the idea of a Creative Spirit do in fact suggest to me, a greater musicality than their English translation. Every time I think about them, a deep sense of connection to a living, breathing universe wells up, enfolding me in its vast musical cloak of wonder and magic.

The Oran Mór is an ancient rhythm, an ancient melody that one hears in the wind, in the waterfall, in the beautiful strains of sound in Celtic music, song and chanting. It is a healing song, an enlivening song heard in the giggles of a grandmother, the whispers of a lover, the questions of a child. All religions would do

well to foster in their followers the same kind of sensual innocence
we had as children, the same kind of curiosity that leads us to ask,
"How do you hear the Great Song in your culture? How do you
hear the Great Song in your religion?" Therein, lies our salvation.
Frank MacEowen, *The Mist-Filled Path*, pp. 140-141, New
World Library 2002

I close my eyes and invite my wandering mind to slow its pace,
to rest a while from its monkey chattering, and experience
the dream. But all the time I am conscious of the silver white
moonlight path that shimmers bright beguiling, between
the Welsh and English Shores. Then, I wait, until the eye of
awareness opens her inner door. This is meditation and it is
pointless to rush, for what will be will be. The unconscious
mind, which only speaks in symbols and archetypes, needs to
be given enough sacred space to fire up the imagination.

Soon, an image of an otherworldly being begins to form in
my mind's eye, which I also see reflected in the outer world of
form, as an effect created by the light of a full moon shining
on a background of night rippling sea. I shall call this ethereal
figure of light an angel for it resembles a cultural image that my
conscious mind has grown up with and can therefore relate to
with ease.

He stands serene all pearly white, in a halo of soft silver and
pale rainbows, as tall as a tree with his feet upon a silvered path
created by the moon. Although he appears to be male, there
is also softness, a feminine quality about him, as he speaks
through my heart and mind in a flow of words as gentle as a
dove yet sharp and clear as a bell.

"I offer you creative wisdom," the angel says, floating in a
circle of candle glow and pale colors that seem to move in tune
with the sound of his voice. "You may not always be aware of
me, but when a door is about to close on one area of your life,
I will always turn up to help you to open a new one, as well as

offering guidance on the next stage of your creative journey. Now, since you are aware of me tonight, then why not stretch your imagination and allow your consciousness to expand?"

The impression of an open door appears before me as if by magic, to reveal a mysterious misty road that extends far away into the distance. It is neither fully formed nor yet clearly visible, for it needs my footsteps to complete the magic.

"Observe the path of your heart and know that as soon as you choose to tread upon it, so the mist will clear." The angel's smile is generous as he adds, "A path that I am hoping you might be inclined to follow, and should you have enough courage to venture out, then I shall be more than happy to accompany you. What do you say? Are you ready?"

And with that, the Universe inside me becomes an entire choir of angels and stars, all singing to the moon and the ocean, penetrating the dark corners of nighttime earth, sky and human mind.

"Slow down now, Angel," I say, feeling far too laid-back to move my mind in any direction. "I am getting older, as you know, though I'm definitely up for an adventure."

The angel responds with another smile, as sweet as honey from a thousand bees. "Whatever you ask, I will oblige, for it is up to you to set the pace. I have forever at my disposal and time does not exist for me."

I take the pearly hand the angel holds out and we head off towards the dawn, still cloaked in muted color and sea mist.

"There is so much music," I tell my companion. "It is forming words, which spiral through my heart and mind in threads of pale gold. I'm afraid if I do not stop to write them down, then I shall soon forget all I have heard."

"Like I said," the angel replies, "time, does not exist for me."

"And like I told you before, Angel, I'm getting older and since I've no idea how much time is left to me, then it is logical that I might sometimes have a tendency towards impatience."

"Impatience speeds time up, and patience slows it down," the angel's gentle reprimand is given without the slightest hint of blame. "Tap into the magic and stop complaining," he adds, "since the Song will continue regardless of how many humans, seasons, creatures, or even worlds may come and go."

And here I am at peace and still again, as my companion continues to hold me in his smile. I take my pen and write until the spinning golden threads of the song have all been woven into lines of words. These words.

He nods. "Have you ever observed," the angel says, as soon as I finish my task, "how the musical instrument you call a harp is fashioned in a similar shape to the human heart?"

"Why yes, it has occurred to me. Maybe it's because I live in Wales or maybe it's an echo from some Irish Celtic gene bequeathed to me from somewhere in my ancestry, or even the strong feeling of connection I experience with the natural world and its landscapes. Harps have an association with both Wales and Ireland, and when I think of harps, then I am reminded of Bards and the stream of inspiration they call *Awen*. Now that is a Welsh word, isn't it?"

"Whatever you call it," my companion answers, "the inspiration is coming from the Oran Mór, which as you know is Gaelic, but although it can be named in any human language, the Great Song can only be understood through softening the heart and listening to the sound that flows through the universe, through all existence. The words are an attempt to describe the sound of becoming, intoned by my kind in our language of angels, and which I am at this moment using to communicate and you are translating, because we are connecting heart to heart. I am therefore flowing through your stream of consciousness as inspiration. To truly understand your part in the Song, it is essential that you tune up your instrument, to become harmonic."

"And shall I always be able to hear you?" I ask, knowing how easily I can get distracted and lose the connection.

"Remember that there is art in your heart, two words that make a rhyme. If you choose to walk upon the path I show you tonight, then you will hear me. Should you become distracted and stray, then all that happens, is you become involved in the world's noise again, the chattering of your own restless wandering mind. As you know, all of that can be discordant, so I don't expect you'll be gone for too long."

"You are right, I do get involved with the noise sometimes, but eventually, it's bound to get on my nerves, and it is then, I'll come looking for you in the quiet places. But tell me, how am I able to translate what you tell me. There are no college courses for learning angel language. It's not exactly like when I learned French at school, or when I signed up for an evening class in Italian is it?"

"When the mind and heart come together, the language of angels is easy to translate. Then you will create with love. Our song is the language of creation, the sound that calls everything into being. The Creative Spirit channels through the angel stream where the energy frequency steps down, so that you can receive and use it. The musical idea of a choir of angels is perfectly compatible with the idea of a Great Song, is it not?"

"The image you are evoking for me feels warm and safe with no hard edges."

"The Great Song is a love song, creation is joyful," the angel continues. "It is the stress in human minds that messes everything up for you and makes harm instead of beauty. The words of the Song translate according to personal creative ability. You are hearing poetry, stories, philosophy, healing, light. Sculptors can see a soul in a block of stone or wood, potters see a vase in a lump of clay, artists see light, color and form on blank canvases, whilst a jeweler might see patterns, symmetry and energy in precious metals and stones. Some humans receive information that translates into wonderful systems, healing medicine, or into machines that enhance life on your planet.

Human diversity is truly amazing, and as a species, you've only uncovered the jewels that lie on the top layer of the deep treasure chest available to you. You must apply love and walk with courage, if you want to be part of the Great Song. We very much hope that your species will not destroy the environment with your discord or indeed, become extinct before you can reach your true potential."

"I begin to understand you," I say still walking at my own pace. "Our minds need light, and our hearts need love. We can learn to give and receive both. We can learn to become a part of everything, to harmonize with the Song, and instead of seeing ourselves as separate dominant creatures, we can take responsibility. It's the separation that causes the craziness, isn't it? We think we are alone," I say, suddenly feeling nurtured, like the angel and the moon are enfolding me in inclusive arms.

"Then you will continue to hear my song," he replies, "for as long as you are prepared to listen. If you write at your own pace, then, there will be peace within and without. No pressure, of course the choice is always yours."

"Thanks," I answer, "I really do want to listen."

I have an impression of silver bells as the angel beams at me, filling the room with profound peace, before his form begins to fade. The words are all written for today. I stand up to close the balcony door and notice that the moonlight has also receded. Although the path across the water has almost vanished, it still exists within my imagination, under my feet and in my heart space, clear and gold now, stretching from shore to shore, alive and shimmering with music from the stars.

Practice

Choose a time of day that appeals to you for making your own creative connection. You might like to set up a small table with a special candle next to an open window, or outside if you have a garden. I use a tall, ornate brass-colored lantern with an electric candle, but it is up to you to choose something that fires your own imagination. You may also wish to buy a notebook with an appealing cover, for recording any impressions or ideas that come to you during this exercise. Let your heart guide you in your choice of these things, but if you prefer to use a phone or a tablet then that is also okay.

Sit comfortably with your back straight, allow your eyes to close and take three slow deep breaths, feeling your mind slow down and your body relax. Now put your awareness into the center of your chest, tuning into your heart center and allowing your energy to expand into the space around you. Pay attention to anything that comes to you through your senses such as an internal image, a sound, a scent, a color, a symbol, light from the sun, the moon or the stars, a sacred object, images from the natural world, the arts etc. You don't have to see an angel, you only need to be open to whatever comes to inspire you. Allow the impressions to flow freely until your communication is complete, then, give thanks for the connection you have experienced.

Now become aware of your breathing again, contract your expanded energy back into your body and imagine drawing a curtain, to close any otherworldly impressions you may have had during this practice. Feel your feet connecting firmly to the ground, flex your fingers and toes before opening your eyes. Record any impressions, ideas and inspiration you have received. Repeat this exercise any time it feels appropriate.

Chapter Two

Inspired

The Language of Angels

There is peace in dove grey mountains
And in this rich red Roman earth
as late October sunshine wraps my skin
in its subtle scent of ripened lemons
the leaves turn slow from green to gold
I see my inspiration like a lighted lamp
and then my mind becoming still at last
is more than just a little glad to be here
in Italy, such a warm embracing place
where my own creative truth out runs
the waves of restless racing thoughts
and the sound of my heart's voice rises
speaking soft in the language of angels.
Iona Jenkins (revised version of original poem in Heartsong, *2016)*

For many years, images of angels have intrigued me, flying through my imagination, clothed in otherworldly splendor, with their warmth and flashes of illumination, evoking whispers of subtler realms existing alongside our everyday reality. Realms that can influence and enhance our lives.

Whether these realms and their inhabitants really do exist or whether they are archetypes in my subconscious, is not too important. The fact is, that my awareness of them as a poet and writer, comes from a type of consciousness that makes me spiritually creative. I am open to all these flowing threads of inspiration, seeking creative expression through my soul, processing their intention in my heart, before moving into my

11

mind, which then begins to weave them into a tapestry of words.

I think that my interest in angels must have begun in the Catholic Church, where art was abundant with their images. I attended services regularly as a child with my great-aunt, who was also my godmother. At that time, the mass was still celebrated in Latin and a heady cloud of incense hung over the congregation every Sunday. I took my first communion in a long white dress at the age of seven, was confirmed at twelve and I remained true to the faith, until friendships became more important, because they opened up new social and developmental possibilities in my early adolescence.

I attended the local village primary school, not the newly opened Catholic one. My parents preferred this option since my mother was not Catholic and neither she nor my father were regular churchgoers. Their marriage had been a civil one followed by a Catholic blessing to appease my grandfather. My godmother, though disappointed, was still my great-aunt regardless of what I chose to do. I duly received an Irish Catholic initiation into my early spirituality, in keeping with the tradition of my father's family and I followed that road until I considered myself old enough, at fourteen, to make my own decision about it. The job had been done and no one objected when I transferred my loyalties to music and dancing.

Although I have been writing poems for many years, it wasn't until around 2008 when I paid an October visit to Italian friends in Rome that I really began to associate not only the arts in general, but also this flow of poetry I received, with the idea of a language of angels. The incredible art, sculptures and history of the Eternal City had touched me as deeply as the light of dawn, or the sun sparkling on the sea outside my small apartment in South Wales. The colors and forms flowed through my soul, set my heart ablaze and sent me running for my notebook and pen. Later, I was to see nature and human art flowing together as sculptures in stone with fountains and lush greenery mingling to create the symphony that is the wonder of Tivoli Gardens.

I was holidaying at the home of Italian friends in the province of Lazio about forty-five minutes from Rome by train, when that first angel poem came to me. On the previous day, I had visited the Sistine Chapel in the Vatican, soaking up the awesome images and colors of Michelangelo's great masterpiece. The colors, of course, have been restored since Michelangelo died in 1564. Maybe, it is because the artist was also a sculptor, the biblical figures on that famous ceiling appear to have a three-dimensional quality, as if they are alive, talking and gesturing from their heavenly world. On the spot, I drafted a reflective piece called "Sistine Chapel" in my notebook. (Published in *Heartsong*, 2016.)

In St. Peter's Basilica, Michelangelo's statue known as *La Pieta* moved me so deeply, I became tearful. This magnificent creation has resided behind protective glass ever since some crazy guy going berserk with a hammer attempted to damage it. My heart aches at the thought, because I can scarcely conceive of anger so great, it would seek to destroy something so incredibly beautiful, so apparently ensouled. It's like a nemesis, an out-of-control shadow, the opposite of an artist's will to create beauty and to enhance the world by doing so. Thankfully, the damage has been restored.

It matters not whether you are religious. Beauty such as Michelangelo created, has exquisite timeless qualities, which can inspire, connect and even raise the awareness of those who care to view it. It is how the artist could see a vision of life encased in a block of marble and then chisel away until that soul was released, to be born and to shine in the world. It was as though I was picking up his vision. The look of compassion on the Madonna's face as she cradles the dead Christ, the body of the son she once gave birth to. The marble appears fluid, moving, expressing both the beauty of Christ's life and the pain of his cruel death in every muscle, bone and sinew chiseled to perfection. This sculpture also evokes for me the presence of a divine feminine, the starry compassionate heart of a loving universal mother who cradles us all at birth, then through our troubled times of life and finally in death as we leave the world behind. In contemplating this statue, then, I can find a sense of safety even through such pain as the artist has captured in his marble.

This kind of sacred art is something else. I have no doubt that it is divinely inspired, but this Holy Creative Spirit doesn't just belong to those who practice Christianity, or indeed to any religion for it is universal. There are treasures within us all, waiting to be released into the world through our inspiration and creative energy. We can all listen to the language of angels and enhance our environment in ways that are small, or great, according to our capacity since everyone's creativity is valuable. We can find that energy in the beauty of earth from which we spring, the life and light of the energizing sun, the intuitive awareness of the mystical moon and the distant mysteries of the stars. Sometimes, we find it in an outpouring of emotion, in human love or in the work of fellow artists. But first, we need to open our senses, learn how to tune in and become aware.

It also seems to me that a truly great sculptor, artist, architect, and poet such as Michelangelo, born during the High Renaissance period, in Caprese, which lies 62km from Florence, was capable of channeling huge blasts of creative force, through an outstanding talent destined to produce works of art that have continued to dazzle us for over four and a half centuries after his death. Infused with the power to ignite imagination and to draw emotion, such works of art are signposts, pointing the way towards a power that is ever greater than the artist himself.

I see this when I look at the central panel on the ceiling of the Sistine Chapel, where God is reaching out to touch Adam's index finger with his own. This panel, known as *The Creation of*

Man, depicts a direct transmission of creative power, a meeting of heaven and earth, a quickening if you like. According to his dates, which Wikipedia gives as 1475-1564, Michelangelo lived to the ripe old age of eighty-eight or nine, an unusually long lifespan for someone of that period. The Force certainly seems to have been with him even though he almost lost his sight, painting for a Pope who constantly delayed payment and gave him a hard time. I wonder whether being named after a well-known Archangel might have had something to do with it.

Journeying on a creative path is no easier than following any other spiritual way, and sometimes beauty and inspiration demand a measure of personal sacrifice. A muse or angel can be insistent, demanding attention in the early hours, when the world is silent. I often wake up with a need to write down words and ideas fast flowing through my mind before I get off to sleep again. I can shelve thinking about a problem until later, but not poetic inspiration. If I do that, it is easily forgotten or lost completely. I would liken this kind of written flow to a wild mountain stream, that cannot easily be contained within the two or three disciplined hours I might dedicate to writing a short story or a chapter of a novel. These streams of beauty, however, can also later enliven description for other kinds of creative writing, after I have understood their place in my poetry.

Italy for me, has been a special place. I have often been personally aware of a quality of light in the cities of Rome and of Florence I have not experienced in any other urban environment. I am not suggesting that it doesn't exist in other cities, only that I have not yet become aware of it. This light quality relates to a sixth sense, I see it with an inner vision, which is then reflected for me in the world outside. Prior to discovering Italy, I had only seen light in rural settings. The noise and bustle of urban landscapes often distracts me, disturbing my peace.

Italy has united angels and the arts for me. Through their masterpieces of painting and sculpture, the imaginations of great artists can connect us to the source from which the Creative Spirit flowed into them. Nowadays, I can also see it in simple art, in writing which is not necessarily going to win great literary acclaim, in ethnic crafts, the physical form of a human body in dance and gymnastics. I hear it not only in the wonderful warmth of a great singing voice such as Andrea Bocelli's, but also in a simple haunting melody, in amateur music, in the enthusiastic creative endeavor that any human being puts their heart and soul into. Some of our artistic efforts may achieve accolades and others may not, but if we are dedicated and sincere, in our intention to enhance the life of others, then the angels will always speak to us.

After I settled in Wales, I became interested in Druids and their concept of Awen, which is symbolized by three bars of light flowing downwards from three dots. This 'Flowing Spirit' describes the language of angels perfectly for me now that my journey crosses Welsh landscapes, evoking memories of Druid storytellers and poets of old, known as Bards. Awen, then, is the Holy or Creative Spirit of the Druids, and when the actual word is sung by a group, the sound produced is empowering. The first time I sang the Awen with others, I could feel my life expanding, as the soaring harmonics created by a group voice invoked impressions of rolling landscapes, green forests, blue seascapes, clear skies and starlit galaxies all unfolding out of the sound.

Singing the Awen, invokes Creative Spirit, raises my awareness, and increases my inspiration because my life shares a resonance with Celtic spirituality and contemporary Druidry. However, I do recognize that we are all remarkably different. There is creative energy to be found in sound options from other practices. For example, in Tibetan Buddhist mantras, the Sanskrit *OM*, repetitions of a prayer from whatever faith. What works to enhance and empower your own spirituality and personal creativity is down to you. Only remember, as you make your personal choices, that it is almost impossible to walk your path, if you happen to be wearing a pair of ill-fitting shoes.

We are all, in general, influenced by our genetics, age, thought processes, country of origin, the area in which we live, our education, social systems and peer groups. I am offering you a map of a spiritually creative journey that comes from my own influences. Nothing is set in stone, as the creative process I am describing is flowing not static. Therefore, I hope my words might just encourage you to dive into your own stream of inspiration, whatever its influences, expressing your creativity through any medium that works best for you.

Practice

Try visiting a gallery, museum, a stately home, church, temple, craft, or antique market, anywhere that offers you an opportunity to spend time studying and connecting with works of art and/or crafts. Try not to think for a few moments, but instead, let your awareness reach out and allow impressions to flow freely through your senses, taking a note of any feelings they evoke, or images they send into your imagination. Eventually, you may wish to choose one or two favorite pieces to work with more deeply.

Be still, breathe deeply, open your heart and connect with form, color and texture.

What is the artist saying to you as an individual?

Note down any idea or realization that comes into your mind.

What stands out for you and why?

Using whatever means of recording information you prefer, make a note of any emotion you might be experiencing.

Any memories from the past or ideas about the future.

Does this art inspire your own creativity in any way?

This exercise can also be done at home using art on a screen, ethnic crafts, favorite objects, family heirlooms, pictures, fabrics, jewelry, listening to music or poetry. Anything that someone else has created, that takes your fancy. By discovering the essence of whatever you have chosen to focus on, you are also connecting to the creative flow that inspired it.

Never underestimate the powerful effect that working with art or sacred objects can have on the imagination, or of the possibilities your inspiration might invoke. A few years ago, in a local creative writing group, I was given a task to choose a favorite object from my home, as a possible source of inspiration for writing.

And I chose a singing bowl that my husband and I had

brought back from Nepal. I loved both its music and form, as well as the fact that it also stirred memories as soon as I lifted it out of the cabinet for dusting. When I tapped the brass-colored metal, the tone of its bell flowed on into a creative spiritual reflection evoked by the sound, my previous experience of Buddhist meditation and my recollection of the Himalayas, covered in snow at New Year. The reflection later appeared in the Writers' and Artists' showcase in *Kindred Spirit Magazine* published by Watkins in May 2018. I have already described how the art I saw in Rome mingled with nature, to become the lines of a poem that in turn inspired this book.

Chapter Three

Song of the Wind

Pine Magic

I paused to rest my back against your bark today
so tall so straight all reddish brown and cracked
from moss hidden roots to sky twisting branch
your long twig fingers are gnarled and pointing
like crooked signposts far away toward the stars
and all those empty spaces stretching far beyond
I could not hope to reach within one human life
except for all the mystic notes you sing to me
your fine green pine magic, ancient, wizard wise
flowing warm through lofty boughs on air streams
an aria so light yet loud, this budding season sound
green and needle sharp in the spring singing sky.
Iona Jenkins

Kew Gardens, a green haven situated by the River Thames on the West London/Surrey border, is certainly inspiring. Fertile and rich with plants and trees from all over the World, this garden is a global horticultural masterpiece. Kew's primary role, of course, is conservation, but for tourists and locals alike, it is also a sanctuary.

In 1986, after moving from Yorkshire to take up a teaching post on the outskirts of London, I met an enthusiastic Welshman with a zest for life and a sense of humor. We married two years later and settled in West London, where we continued to live and work for a quarter of a century. We also became friends of Kew Gardens, so that our membership not only provided us with green space for regular walking, meditation, and inspiration, it also contributed to conservation and plant research.

That friendship was one of the best relationships I have ever experienced. There was a sense of soul soothing and relaxation every time I walked through any one of the three visitors' gates. As time passed, I found my own favorite contemplation spots. The landscape, cultivated into various horticultural themes, seemed like an enormous open-air dwelling place, composed of many rooms, each with its own unique atmosphere with sights and scents according to the season.

For instance, I loved the grove of giant redwoods with their thick, squashy, rust-colored bark. Now, I don't exactly go around hugging trees, but I did discover that leaning against one of these tall stately beings would always give me a sense of strength, stability and grounding. I also found a place of bluebells in May, where the depth of color and a perfume like heaven, filled my senses and made my heart glad, whenever I took the time to contemplate their flower carpet splendor. Finally, I recall the powerful aroma of sun-warmed pine resin on a hot day under the trees, just beyond the big lake. The smell was like incense burning in a shady green nature temple, and I just loved to breathe such heady perfume from nature's woody censer fired by the sun, because it always felt so joyful and holy.

Crisp cold winters were as interesting as balmy summers. The Palm House and the tropical Princess of Wales Conservatory provided warmth when the landscape was covered in silver grey mist, freezing the still air and dormant earth. In spring, the Rhododendron Dell flowered in purples, pinks and whites like colored silks and the autumn brought delicate red maple leaves, translucent as glass, for the sun to illuminate.

When my husband had to work on Saturday, I explored many beautiful spots along the River Thames alone, but Kew always remained my favorite. On one such Saturday, I entered Kew Gardens through the Lion Gate, then walked across the grass in a direct line from the Pagoda. A smooth green lawn with a wide vista, opened out on to a small lake with a Dove Cote. There were usually peacocks, either strutting around the water's edge or wandering through the surrounding trees. Opposite the lake, memorial benches provided a resting place beneath a row of tall Scots Pines.

This early spring day was breezy and comfortable for walking, but too cool to take my coat off. As usual, I sat down on one of the benches, concentrated on my breath and allowed my awareness to blend into the nature all around me. It was then, I registered a strong impression of the wind, as it coursed through the branches high above my head. I had heard it many times before, but it had never entered my consciousness in quite the same way as on that day. Well at least not in my adult life. I was in one of those magic moments, when both body and mind slow down, when time seems to stand still, as awareness refines and expands. The wind, the moving branches, the sunshine appearing, then suddenly vanishing in blue skyscapes, ever changing in the drifting of white clouds. Then, the water, a peacock cry, the space above the clouds where my soul could soar to almost touch the stars, even in daylight.

In more recent years I have understood that a tall pine will often point me towards the stars. That may be a personal thing, so I will have to leave it up to you, my readers, to seek out your own pines and test out the experience for yourselves.

As I continued to listen to those Kew pines, I began to experience a deep resonance with this music of the wind in the trees that seemed to exist not only outside in the garden, but inside me as well. I placed my palm against my chest and felt my heart beating with the sound of my life, harmonic with the wind and rustling pines. Was this an experience of the sound of creation? Was this a note from the Great Song that Celtic wisdom refers to as the Oran Mór? This wind song had no words, but the sound combined with the effect of sunlight bursting intermittently through blue sky gaps left by scudding clouds, brought me a vision of a golden harp with rippling strings moving in time and in tune with the air.

The image in my mind's eye changed to add a harpist, an angel figure robed in pale blue light. The scene reminded me of a picture on an old music tape I used to have, an image that has remained imprinted on my memory for many years. Golden harps and angels are two important personal symbols for me, though I do not associate them with any kind of religious heaven. The image of an angel playing a harp is leading me towards the idea of angels as something energetic, a subtle but integral part of the creative force. I am beginning to understand their language in terms of color, and sound.

Science provides its own way to describe our beginnings, but since I am an artist, I find sound, words, color, and movement very appealing. Before we understood the world in scientific terms, we would use our imaginations to tell creation stories. That being the case, I let the words in the stream of inspiration flow through my imagination and form what they will. That is how I see my own sensory image of the Creative Force or Spirit, how I interpret the concept of a language of angels or the sound of the Awen.

I remember how I first heard that angel language whilst playing outside in the green as a child in touch with my wild soul. I heard it carried on the air rustling or rushing through the wise old trees, whenever I lay in the grass breathing flower scents or lazing by the gurgling stream watching darting sticklebacks. I found real enjoyment and wonder in the sound of bees buzzing and birds singing in the natural world with myself happy and laughing at the center of it all. Kew brought my magic child back to me and encouraged me to listen with my heart again.

Practice

Locate a place outside in nature where it is possible to sit and tune in to the landscape around you and the sky above your head. Make sure that the place you have chosen is also safe. You will need a small notebook or a phone to record your experience. Native American shamans used to leave gifts of tobacco in sacred places. I am not a smoker, nor do I care for the smell of it, so I choose to leave dried pink rosebuds instead. These are easy, light to carry and the scent is glorious. Decide for yourself whether you want to leave a gift and what that gift will be. Speaking or chanting a few words or projecting images of peace might feel appropriate to some, rather than an actual physical gift. Whatever you decide to do, remember that this small ritual is a way of showing respect to your chosen environment. Learning this skill will also encourage you to find self-respect.

You are now about to befriend your chosen sacred place, so to begin, find somewhere to sit or stand and pay attention to whatever comes to you through your senses. Become aware of the trees and plants, then any animals, birds or insects that might be around keeping you company. Take notice of the season, the time of day, the color of the sky, the position and strength of the sun, the weather, and the temperature, in the same way as when you connect to your inner world. Now, however, your eyes are open, and you are working outwards in the world of form.

How does your body feel? How are you emotionally? If your feelings are distracting you, don't try to cut them off, rather acknowledge them kindly, as part of your experience and they will more than likely begin to relax their grip on your mind much sooner. Be prepared to attempt this task more than once before you feel aligned with the landscape. Continue to remind yourself that you are still a part of it even when you are not feeling totally in tune. Eventually you will come back into harmony as your connection becomes stronger.

Attuning to the natural world brings a sense of communication, which for an artist may turn into inspiration. Some people sit or walk outside when they need to think clearly, to solve problems, and perhaps by doing so, they get more help than they realize.

When you feel your connection coming to a natural end for today then give thanks to this place for welcoming you and returning your friendship. Record any impressions you have received. If you should experience any significant heightening of awareness during this exercise, then make sure to imagine that you are drawing a curtain across your experience or maybe closing a door before you leave, so that you are fully grounded. If you do not feel resonant with the images I have suggested for closing, then experiment to discover what works best for you as an alternative.

File any notes you consider important for future reference. Sometimes these exercises create ideas that become useful later.

Chapter Four

The Well and the Ocean

Sea Misty Morning

An early morning sea fret
descends like damp ghosts
on breeze fluttering leaves
and pale waning moonglow
in a grey water colour sky
Cardiff Bay twinkles muted
fairy lights behind the mist
there is no seagull soaring
or notes of chorus dawning
for the birds are still asleep.
Iona Jenkins

I wake up at 5am. There are significant changes going on in my life and I not sure yet where those changes are taking me. Relinquishing control and letting go can be a wrench, even when I know I must move on. The leap of faith required, feels like a threat to my security, though I have a deep gut feeling there is no longer any security left for me in a situation, which is using more energy than I can afford to give right now. I need to let go, to accept and finally settle into my own creative life, to stop looking for extra responsibility. It has become necessary to acknowledge my own vulnerability, because I need some space to heal, I need energy and inspiration to write, to put out what is welling up inside me.

I open my box of 12 Chalice Well Essences and take 7 drops of the one labelled Trinity of Holy Thorn, which is supposed to help with major life changes. I am all set to stride out on my own, though right now my life has a lot in common with this ghostly morning full of sea mists, where the earth is cloaked, where the edges are all blurred, and nothing appears totally distinct.

I finish the poem I am working on and decide to go back to bed. I am aware of the birds now, as I glance at the clock on my bedside table. It is 5:45am and I can hear the first screeching of gulls. I fall asleep again and do not awake until almost 8.

Two hours on, the energy has changed, letting a brighter atmosphere into my world, an awareness of light surrounding me, stimulating my mind. I think about the moonlight angel. Now that question of whether he is an archetype inhabiting my psyche or whether he exists in a separate subtle dimension overlapping this one, may continue to remain open to some debate, but in the end, encounters with him not only increase my energy, but they also certainly inspire me and sometimes heal, so all is in fact well. With this thought, the light becomes pearl white again, infused with pastel rainbows.

"Don't question it," I sense the angel saying, as his presence becomes more distinct. "Why don't you just relax and accept the experience? It will not unbalance you. In fact, I would say that you look much more harmonious than you did when you first awoke at 5 o'clock."

"You are right," I reply, "when you are around, I stop wasting my energy, getting anxious or uppity about things I can't control. In fact, my head feels totally clear right now and I'm anchored in the present. I felt unwell when I woke up earlier, but the Chalice Well remedy and the moon waning in the early morning mist, seem to have sent me back to you."

"That essence works for you because it is exactly the right one, taken at the right time. That's how the magic of these things tends to operate. You cooperate instead of fighting."

"The pain in my shoulders has eased," I say, rolling them around a little. "As you know I've been having physiotherapy for my shoulders and my right arm."

"Let go, and let me in," the angel answers without the slightest hint of impatience. "You are moving on, leaving a situation that is no longer right for you, though it may indeed now suit someone else. You have done as much as you can and you are passing work on, so that another person can have an opportunity to grow from watering the seeds you have sown and then planting some more of their own. Change is inevitable since the universe does not stand still. Worlds are created, they live out their time, they die, and new ones take their place. You are about to enter a new phase of understanding and you are discovering new purpose. You are experiencing growing pains."

"Growing pains! And here's me thinking it's arthritis. The pain has certainly caused me some restrictions recently. The physio is helping. I intend to continue with the exercises because they are preferable to surgery."

"Call it what you like and please continue to exercise, as you are getting positive results from doing that. However, in this moment, I am still inclined to describe your problem as growing pains, so if you relax and allow the process, then you might be able to find some ease and move through it. Stress and tension make the pain worse, don't you find?"

"They certainly do. And by the way, Angel, in my mind's eye, my inner vision, I can see several other light beings much like yourself only smaller. They seem to be forming out of the pale colors I can see around you."

"They are all aspects of creative and healing energy," he replies, "angels with specific purposes if you like and yes, they are different colors. We are all part of the same Creative Spirit. We are one and yet we also exist in our own right."

"I know you said not to question it, Angel, but I would really like you to tell me whether you are an archetype, an image in my unconscious mind, or whether you exist outside of me?"

"Then the answer to your question is both," he replies. "You have a postcard on your bookcase do you not? It has a quote from the Buddha who once said, 'It is your mind that creates the world.'"

"Yes, I keep it close to a rose quartz crystal. To me the beautiful rose stone reminds me of the qualities of love and kindness. It feels heart centered."

"Now you have it," he laughs. "Last time we talked, I told you that our connection is heart to heart. The heart adds loving kindness to whatever world your mind can create, and it is important to remember that. Clear-cut crystal especially diamond, might represent a heart-influenced mind to you, brilliant and filled with light. Perhaps you may find time to explore what different crystal forms mean to you. You are noticing how much interaction with the world is colored by what you choose to focus on. You are learning to live your life as an artist, and by the way, writing is a powerful art form."

"Yes," I agree, "a member of my writing circle once observed how authors have the power to create characters and then destroy them if they feel like it."

"Authors and poets observe life, they record significant events, and they certainly have the power to influence others, to open the doors of possibility with their words. We can provide a voice for change and growth through them. Is there any wonder fear-based repressive regimes sometimes resort to persecution and book burning to silence that voice? Yes, writing is powerful. Especially since thoughts create the world, whether as a story in a book or in real life events across the globe. Every ounce of positive energy emitted, every positive thought or act goes some small way to changing the whole. Sometimes you take a risk in doing that."

"Which brings me back to the rose quartz. When I lived in London, I heard about a Buddha in waiting, a Buddha for the next age, who is supposed to succeed Shakyamuni the present Buddha of Compassion. This one is known as Maitreya, the Buddha of Loving Kindness. Although I cannot in all honesty call myself a Buddhist, I do feel a resonance with certain aspects of those teachings. I am sure that Loving Kindness is a quality the world needs right now."

The angel looks pleased, "See how you made that association. Why not leave the seed to germinate and sprout. It might grow into another creative idea in the fertile soil of your imagination. Changes are already happening. There are many, especially amongst the young, who are beginning to speak out about the damage to the environment of your planet."

"Thanks, I'll give that association some thought. I certainly feel empathy with the efforts of young people who want to take responsibility for protecting the environment of a world they are set to inherit," I reply. "But returning to creative activity now, I am considering painting two pictures. One involves you and the moon. The other has more color and the smaller angels around you. Technically, I am not much of a painter, as I have no sense of perspective or talent with form, though I do enjoy working with color. I'm much better at painting with words."

"You don't have to be Michelangelo," the angel smiles kindly, "you just need to translate what comes to you in whatever way you can. His purpose was very specific, and at that time, we worked with his talent to inspire in a big way and his work is still doing that. Your own efforts may yet be useful along with your writing. In your case it's the energy contained in your pictures rather than the actual forms. Do you have a word to describe your current life experience?"

"Yes, the word is *transition* and the first time we spoke I thought of *connection*."

"If further inspiration should come your way regarding these words, then write down all the different associations that occur around them."

"This transition has been painful in more than one sense of the word, but as soon as I become aware of you, I feel connected and there is no pain at all," I continue.

"The transition has been going on for roughly nine months and some of the pain you have experienced has its origins in the past. It happens, you know, pain from the past latches on to similar triggers in the present and augments that experience. You would do well to let go and trust in the truth of your own life. Try to stop blaming yourself and others, stop using fear, insecurity or regret to push against the current. It's a learned human response that is obviously exhausting. When you reach the end of a journey, rest awhile, then simply open the next door so that you can create a new path as you walk."

"You make it sound so simple! I am tired and feeling fragile." I look at him through misty eyes.

"Then honor that fragility," he says, bringing his gentle presence closer for security. "I know you have had to find a great deal of strength in the past, but it really was in the past, so let the situation, the people and the work go. The good will remain with you and you do not need to hold on to any of the baggage. If you keep a box full of useless old stuff, then how can you put any bright new things in it?"

"That's obvious," I snap. "Why do I persist in being stupid?"

"Don't insult yourself, you're human," he answers, "and humans have a lot to learn. Wisdom takes time to develop, wouldn't you agree?"

I smile, because this angel has such patience and I never receive the slightest hint of blame for anything from him. I offer a reminder that I am a Companion of Chalice Well in Glastonbury, England and that I am planning to go there on the following weekend.

"The first time I ever became aware of angels in nature, I was in Chalice Well Gardens. Did you know that?" I ask him.

"Of course, it's a place where you really connect, though you were not aware of me specifically at that time. Why not top up your supply of Chalice Well essences, as they do seem to help you. This transition will be complete before your birthday."

"I went to Snowdonia on my birthday last year, but I haven't quite decided what to do this year."

"Wait until after a new moon before you make any decisions, as the path is sometimes clearer when the moon is waxing."

"You don't work with me through the sun, do you?" I ask him.

"Well, it's daylight now is it not? I have been working with the moon and the element water, through your intuitive mind, as you are always drawn to the ocean outside your window, but it is early days yet. You may soon discover that we are able to communicate in a variety of places and situations. This is your dream after all, so it is up to you to make those decisions and to create the opportunities."

"That makes sense, but although I am so often drawn to the moon with the sea, I also connect to starlight or sunlight shining on the water outside my window. Thinking about it, I suppose that the intuitive feminine moon softens and reflects sunlight. Chalice Well, which is very special to my heart, is also a water place. I am experiencing a need to flow more with life like the water flowing into the well."

"Just so," the angel agrees, "and the Chalice Well in its wonderful garden, provides a peaceful sanctuary for all manner people, whatever their beliefs may be. Your own decision to go there is a decision to trust in your own process, to understand for yourself in terms of what works for you and what does not."

When the angel finishes his sentence, I see a signpost in my own process, pointing towards the Sacred Feminine. I experience a softening, a stronger sense of flow as once again I am reminded of the art in Rome. At that moment, the sun bursts out from behind the clouds and the wind picks up, bringing me back to the world of my conscious mind, though I am still aware of the colors from the otherworldly realm and the loving kindness of the angels who inhabit it.

Questioning whether all of this exists inside or outside of

me, suddenly has no importance. Inside and outside now appear to be two halves of the same whole, with the outside reflecting that which exists inside and vice versa. At the center, we can all encounter our original innocence, our original goodness, to form a balance to the old idea of original sin some of us have been overfed on. We feel enough strength to assume responsibility for our own shadows, whenever we realize that we are supported within the creative heart of a loving, nurturing and compassionate universe. If everyone was able to illuminate the world outside with a reflection of their original goodness, then the scales would tip into balance, and change would surely happen.

I lie down on the sofa for five minutes, melting into the wind, the light over the water and the landscape. There is a sense of peace and healing, a sense of balm for the soul. I have no urge to go anywhere. Today is a time for being not doing, a time to relax into this transition and allow all worldly events to take their course.

Practice

Sit comfortably, close your eyes, and allow your memory to drift back to somewhere that felt special to you, a place that really fired your imagination. If you felt a spiritual connection to this site or an emotional resonance with it then that is a bonus.

Next, picture yourself reconnecting to your chosen place as it exists in the inner world of your imagination. Picture yourself walking around it, taking in its special landmarks and features.

What stands out for you in terms of color, light, sound, substance, scent and taste? What does this memory evoke for you? Take all the time you need to explore this place as it exists in your internal world.

Notice any kind of inspiration that arises for you from your chosen place. Does it move your hands to create in any way, your feet to dance, your voice to speak, sing or write? What kind of expression does it ask of you?

When you feel that your exploration is complete, then pull back and detach yourself from the memory, becoming aware of your present surroundings again. Take notes on all your ideas and impressions to use either now or later.

For anyone interested in vibrational essences, there are numerous brands to choose from. The Bach Flower Remedies can be bought in many health-food stores and some chemists. Chalice Well essences are available from the site shop or online at: https://www.chalicewell.org.uk/chalice-well-shop/. Do some Internet research of your own on different essences to determine which ones you feel resonant with.

Chapter Five

Sacred Pathways

The Labyrinth

The words that flowed in beauty felt so holy
when slow and sure I made my pilgrim's way
towards the still and quiet centre of a labyrinth
where both the road and I became the same
and nothing else seemed too important then
except to merge in friendship, light and peace
with all who walked this winding path before
falling deeply into love as I enter the centre
a golden heart beating in rainbows of sound.
Iona Jenkins

A labyrinth has a single winding path leading into its center. The same path leads out again and there are no dead ends. A maze on the other hand has more than one path and several dead ends. The two are often confused. Labyrinths come in different shapes and sizes. The two most common types are known as classical and mediaeval. The classical labyrinth has been around for thousands of years, and although there is little certainty about its actual use in the spiritual lives of our ancestors, it is apparent that it may have played a significant role in the beliefs and rituals of some of those ancient peoples. Examples of this flowing design have been found, all over the world, marked on the ground, carved on rocks, or used as decoration on ancient artefacts. The same shape occurs in nature in the form of spirals, shells, fossils, spider webs, which all provide us with examples of such patterns. A classical labyrinth might have 3, 5 or 7 circuits.

Labyrinths became popular in the Christian religion during mediaeval times and the one in the gothic cathedral of Chartres in France is probably the most famous example of a mediaeval labyrinth. The Christian cathedral of Chartres, however, is built over a former Druid site, an ancient well, which suggests a strong link to the sacred feminine.

> *The Cathedral, a quintessential symbol of mediaeval Christianity, is actually built over a pagan shrine, a holy well in a grotto that tradition claims, was a sacred site of the Druids. The ancient Celts worshipped water as a source of life and in particular wells and springs that bubbled out of the ground. Like milk flowing from the breast, they saw the life-giving water flowing from the body of Mother Earth.*
> **Philip Carr-Gomm, *Sacred Places*, p. 96, Quercus 2008**

The Chartres-style mediaeval labyrinth has a more complex design. Laid into the floor of the cathedral's nave in 1201, the center in the shape of a six-petaled rose is reached by following an eleven-circuit path, winding its way through four quadrants.

Some labyrinths in France were constructed during the time of the Crusades when pilgrimages to Jerusalem proved impossible because of the fighting. The path of the Chartres Labyrinth, then, is a symbolic road towards the sacred rose at the center of a New Jerusalem, which I interpret as that internal holy sanctuary, where Christ/Spirit reaches out to touch the hearts of pilgrims and make all creation new.

Labyrinths were popular until around the late 15th century after which they began to decline. Many were destroyed during the 18th and 19th centuries when they were overtaken by the more fashionable garden mazes.

Labyrinths are now exciting interest again, appearing in cathedrals, as well as retreat centers, schools, universities, and convents. Finger labyrinths can also be purchased for contemplation at home. As the index finger is used to follow the path, this kind of hand walking makes the labyrinth accessible to people with mobility issues, in addition to serving as an individual meditation tool or ritual for anyone else. I love to create an atmosphere for finger labyrinth meditation by lighting a candle, or burning incense, reading a poem or prayer, before tracing the path carved into the silken polished wood of my own oaken finger labyrinth.

Meditation is about looking inwards, finding the center. In reaction to life's problems, we are often tempted to turn our attention outwards, even run away, but by walking the labyrinth it is as though we are journeying through our own inner landscape, facing our issues by trusting in this spiritual heartland. A sensation of slowing down, followed by a feeling of peace was a common experience amongst labyrinth walkers I worked with. This peace may offer a spiritual presence that works in accordance with individual beliefs, sufficient space to pray, meditate, or to receive creative inspiration, solutions to important life issues, comfort in times of sorrow, and sometimes even healing. As this wisdom inhabits the creative center of a human being, the labyrinth is a way to connect to our own hearts, from where we hope one day, to gain access to the heart of creation.

There is no right or wrong way to walk labyrinths since they meet us exactly where we are at any given time. When I first encountered this walking meditation on my personal journey, I was about to enter a new creative period in my life. My husband and I had reached a transition both individually and as a couple. We had to go with it, as we were both exhausted. My husband's health problems combined with a loss of income had left us little choice. Pushing against that current would only have added to our burdens and increased that exhaustion. During my last two years in London, then, I had begun to discover my life as a sacred path, with doors to open at significant intervals. I had also begun to embrace the creative process by setting foot on a way of words that would ultimately help me to negotiate some very difficult life circumstances.

Whilst nature and art inspired me, walking labyrinths provided a symbolic path to the center of myself, to the sanctuary of the heart where angels speak and sing the world into being according to the will of a Creative Spirit.

Nature and art became signposts pointing in the direction of my own creativity. They connected me to the Great Song and showed me how to translate the language of angels into poetry, prose, stories, philosophical writing, course material and an occasional brightly colored naïve picture or symbol. I discovered a local meditation teacher, then a Tibetan Buddhist Centre where I deepened my meditation practice, and finally, I came across a one-day labyrinth workshop held at the London Spirituality Centre. After attending the workshop and walking my first labyrinth, set into the paving, right in the heart of the City of London, I knew I was hooked.

Soon after, the connections began to flow with amazing synchronicity, as intention began to color my life. I now realize that I had fallen into the musical moving stream of Awen, where I first encountered the Sacred Feminine. I was shown a simple labyrinth created around a churchyard in West London. Next, I discovered a church in Hampstead where a walk was held every month on a portable canvas eleven-circuit Chartres-style labyrinth. Finally, I was told about the seven-circuit traditional labyrinth in the beautiful Peace Garden situated behind a convent in Ham between Richmond and Kingston on Thames. The Sisters there were happy to accommodate me, when I knocked on their door, eagerly asking if I might have permission to walk their labyrinth on a regular basis.

This sacred path marked out in stones upon the grass, became a fortnightly ritual, through every season, during those last two difficult years in London. When I first entered the garden, it was bursting with fresh bright tulips, daffodils and blossoms in spring, alive with birdsong. At harvest time, ripe fruit fell from the trees and miniature maple leaves glowed translucent red, as the season moved through autumn. Sometimes I would take off my shoes, just to feel support from the good earth through the soles of my feet. Maintaining a strong connection to earth is important during times of difficulty and change, because we need nurture from the great mother we are all privileged to share. Connecting to the stars with our feet firmly rooted in her ground, assures a sense of balance, helps us to remember that we are all part of this wonderful creation, that we are not alone.

As I walked, then recorded my experiences in a notebook, my life became more intuitive, as ideas and milestones flowed into each other with remarkable synchronicity. At certain times in our lives, mother-wit serves us better than intellect. Reconnecting to my own sacred feminine was like returning to the woods and fields of my childhood. I began to walk the labyrinth with creative intent. The words poured out of me in streams of simple wisdom sayings, philosophical ideas and poetry. I found myself inspired with story by secret places along the Thames, which I began to call my magic river. The world became a chalice overflowing with stars, as my reading embraced the poetry of Rumi and Tagore.

At that time, I was working as a secondary school counsellor for three days a week and in private practice during the remaining two weekdays in addition to some evenings. The labyrinth and its garden, combined with the many other magical places I had found along the banks of the Thames, always gave me enough space to be myself, with enough energy left over to help others, even amidst the chaos invading my own life.

There had been personal tragedy and bereavement, we were struggling to make ends meet, my husband, having lost his work, finally began to succumb to illness and needed hospital appointments. In addition to all of that, some of our personal relationships were becoming strained, as we struggled to survive a veritable avalanche of stress that seemed to be falling on us from all directions. Even though I experienced considerable anxiety and emotional upheaval, in the end, I turned out to be much more resilient than I could ever have previously imagined. Looking back on that time, I am grateful for the emotional and moral support I received from a few loyal friends and colleagues, as well as a local meditation teacher and my wonderful very experienced counselling supervisor who kept my feet on the ground and kept me working.

Sometimes adverse life circumstances are signposts telling us to change direction. The glaring signposts on my sacred path were pointing towards the way out of London, away from the need to keep struggling to maintain a lifestyle we no longer needed. We decided to move to Wales, my husband's country of origin, and downsize to have much lower outgoings and to trust that our path would eventually lead us on in the right direction.

First, it led me into taking my pension and an earlier retirement than I had intended, because I hadn't enough spare energy or space in our temporary one-bedroomed flat in Wales to start a new practice. It also led my husband to a hospital bed, surgery, then two further years of recovery time, so he too was forced to slow down and retire. As he began to recover, we found a larger apartment, with a guest room that doubled as a study. I packed up again, got the remainder of our belongings out of storage and we moved. The larger rooms of our new home gave us much-needed space, but the best thing about it was its spectacular view across the Bristol Channel. We made a wise decision to settle here, and now my husband is not only well again, he enjoys better health than he ever had in London, so I am sure we have done the right thing. The sea with its salt air has proved to be a great healer, as well as a great inspirer.

We had freedom for the first time in years. Life became smaller in some ways, but also slower, less expensive, creative, and more relaxed. I found another local Buddhist Centre for meditation and mindfulness in Cardiff. On one of our regular trips to visit my mother and brother, a priest in Lincoln Cathedral told us about a beautiful permanent labyrinth in the garden of a Franciscan retreat center, not far from my mother's house I could walk whenever I visited her. One labyrinth seemed to lead on to another, until finally, I was asked if I would like to facilitate labyrinth workshops for a Christian spirituality group. For the next four years, I became the keeper and facilitator of a five-circuit portable canvas labyrinth.

I have discovered that the labyrinth has mystical qualities, a spiritual intelligence of its own. Drumming up enthusiasm for this more feminine approach to spirituality in traditional church congregations proved very difficult at first, but then, as the energy in the labyrinth grew, so interest increased, as its sacred path reached out to more people. Now, some Welsh schools as well as churches are keen to work with the portable labyrinth, and there is a permanent labyrinth in the grounds of one Cardiff Secondary School.

Last summer I finally embraced change and passed on my role of Labyrinth Keeper. My path was to simplify further, to become more personally creative. I am prone to arthritis and my shoulders and back were painful, which made the equipment cumbersome and heavy. In addition to that my mother's health had begun to deteriorate and I was forced to acknowledge a feeling of exhaustion yet again. It seemed as if my body was telling me to stop. I had packed up my life in London, moved to Wales and my companion in life had been seriously ill, but as usual, desperate to feel secure again, I had gone out and found as many things to do as possible, instead of slowing down into the flow. I now had to acknowledge the enormity of the change we had been forced to make and take a little more time out to adjust to this new life. Finally, listening to the complaints of both body and soul, I decided to stop taking on so much responsibility for others and to settle down into my art, allowing nature to nourish me, as she always has in times of trouble.

I see the body as a vessel for Creative Spirit, to be respected and taken care of. The sacred path was winding into a new way of being for me, and the gift of an angel presence from moon and water in the natural world outside my window, helped me to write the following prescription for my own emotional and physical healing. I sat on my balcony, connecting to the nurturing feminine, through the landscape, the sky and the sea with words pouring into my mind.

"It is time to let go of all this doing for now, to be with the land, the sea and sky, the sun, the moon and the bright stars. It is time to sit on the earth, to talk to her creatures, to change with the seasons. It is time to walk along the sand, on the edge of the waves, to tell your stories to the wind, to heal yourself with quiet time and with natural fare. It is time to breathe deeply and experience the magic of this whole creation, floating in a stream of Awen. All of this can be you in the now, slower, more deliberate, open, in touch, at peace, writing in the flow of Spirit."

That I was able to introduce others to the magic and peace of labyrinth walking, is an achievement, something to celebrate. Now, there are new teachers and facilitators, to water the seeds that have been sown. I hope that they too are listening to their angels. For once, I had found enough wisdom to let go before the going got tough and forced it. My shoulders and left knee are now almost pain free. Giving thanks for all the good people I had met on the path during my time as a Labyrinth Keeper, I moved on, because it was time to do so.

So, where exactly am I going now? The Labyrinth helped me to awaken faith in my own life and my ability to allow the connections to happen, as I make my spiritually creative way, which for now continues to meander through the landscapes of Wales.

Listening to the angels with all my heart, the words carry on flowing into each new chapter of my life, in much the same way as they have flowed into each new chapter of this book.

Practice

If you are not already familiar with labyrinths and would like to learn more about them, then you might find the following resources useful:

Courses and information are available from Veriditas, see veriditas.org which is based in the United States, but also runs courses in the UK and Europe.

The World-Wide Labyrinth Locator shows the location of permanent labyrinths for actual walks and can be found at labyrinthlocator.com.

The Labyrinth Society at https://labyrinthsociety.org has information as well as picture downloads of both classical and Chartres-style labyrinths in their resources section, which can be used for finger labyrinth work.

The Etsy website sells a large selection of finger labyrinths made from wood as well as other materials.

Finally, remember that the labyrinth meets you where you are. If you would like to use the labyrinth to increase your creative connection, then begin each walk with that intention. If you are already working on a project, you can ask for guidance and inspiration before you enter its sacred paths. I have rarely left the labyrinth empty-handed, though sometimes inspiration began small and grew over a period of days. From time to time, I also found myself drawn to relevant books or divination cards. The labyrinth seems to generate an organized energy that enables life to work in greater synchronicity. You can also enter the labyrinth with the intention of seeking healing for yourself or another, asking for guidance and help in decision making or for solving difficult life issues. It can be used for prayer or contemplating the scriptures of any religion. The circular paths and the center are a wonderful sanctuary for those who are simply looking for peace. I like to combine the spiritual with the artistic, and I have seen how such a combination can also facilitate finding answers to problems, as well as triggering certain types of healing. As always, your path and your intent are your own responsibility.

Chapter Six

Words and Alchemy

On Wings of Light

The blue grey lull of the sea at twilight
horizon's shore lamps twinkle into night
as the thin mist curtain opens like a veil
I breathe in stars and fly on wings of light
Iona Jenkins

The tide is out, the shore visible, as I sit looking out over the trees growing on the edge of the cliff. It has been a day of exceptionally clear light, when this clifftop shoreline place, I inhabit in the everyday world, seems to be merging with a mystical Otherworld, a realm existing beyond the earth-functioning level of awareness, firing my imagination with words, colors, and a sense of something so beautiful and so much greater than myself, that it takes my breath away. This happens now and again for no apparent reason, when I am relaxing alone, and then the veil between the conscious world and this subtle world of my intuitive mind seems to melt away.

At night I light the candle in my lantern, so that the flame flickers just inside the doorway to the balcony, which for me has become a threshold place. The weather has been so warm and relaxing that the door has been left open all day, bringing the outside in, filling my front room with seagull cries and wave music.

The threshold idea originates with my Celtic ancestors, druids and shamans, who believed the shores of lakes and oceans to be magical places, where it is possible to glimpse the Otherworld and to receive messages from it. I can certainly go along with such a belief, as moving into this apartment has tripled my passion and inspiration for writing poetry.

In this place, I can achieve a spontaneous meditative state, where pictures flood my imagination and words flow in what I see as a circular clockwise motion. The sound of my poetry sometimes seems to have a spiraling shape, though I write the actual words on paper in straight lines. Sometimes, I might open my mouth to speak those words before I write, as they form themselves into a poem, a philosophical meandering or question and answer sessions with an angelic image or bright being. I have never tried storytelling in the oral tradition, but I can't think why that wouldn't work in the same way for anyone who is talented in that way.

The entrance to a forest or wood is also a threshold, which takes me into a different domain, where the trees exist in a vast underground network of root formations, with their crowns reaching skyward to absorb sunlight through their leaves. In the spirit of a wandering deer, I look upon woodland as a haven, a place to shelter, a place of life force and well-being, somewhere I feel welcome.

Observing a shamanic tradition of leaving gifts, I carry a small pouch of dried rosebuds in my cross-body bag whenever I go out into nature or visit a sacred site. The village of Woodhall Spa is surrounded by woodland. This is where I enjoy going for walks combined with writing, whenever I visit my mother and brother, who both now live, in rural Lincolnshire.

Two of the greatest hurdles creative people often face are rejection and criticism not only from the world outside, but also from their own internal critics. Opinions may be based on market forces, or they may be entirely subjective. What we really need is constructive feedback. I share my first drafts with a small writing circle, or friends who have enough respect to look at my work objectively, and help me make improvements, rather than destroying what I have created. As the angel indicated earlier, severe rejection or criticism from the past can get mixed up with work criticism or even emotional memories, historical stuff that has nothing to do with creativity in the present. Criticism of our art may occasionally trigger unresolved memories of personal slights from years ago, thus digging up a heap of buried rubbish. We've all been criticized and rejected.

Those who have borne harsh criticism for a long time, so often fail to hear or register the genuine praise they receive. Paying attention, accepting and noting all the positive feedback and praise given, can help to alter perception in such a way, that a new shining thread becomes visible in the tapestry, bright enough to add a positive line to the story, thus making a difference to the structure of the plot.

On one such day, when I was feeling particularly vulnerable, somewhat stunned after receiving what I considered to be very unjust criticism, I arrived at the entrance to the wood. With my mind whirring away, I walked right past a familiar beech tree, a tall guardian standing just inside the threshold. I don't know why or how, but it was like some kind of force stopped me in my tracks. I stood still, almost rooted to the spot, as my focus altered in an instant. I turned slowly to look at the towering beech and straight away realized that wallowing in my rejected thoughts was preventing me from enjoying the experience of the present moment. I had forgotten to leave my usual gift for the guardian tree spirit at the entrance to the wood. As soon as I reached into my bag for a dried rosebud to place on the ground and turned my attention towards the tree, the following idea started circling around my imagination.

"The word you need first is *PRAISE* so think about the opposite to all the stuff that's been bothering you. Think *WORTHY* instead of unworthy, *ACCEPTANCE* instead of rejection. Create some balance in your mind. Concentrate on your heart center as you think about and intone these words. Put colors and images with them if you feel like it. Criticism is okay if it's valid and given generously as honest feedback without any personal agenda. You need to weigh that up for yourself and act accordingly. Do not mix these feelings with stuff from the past. Be present in your body and take responsibility for your own life. The attitudes of others are more likely to change when you change the critic in yourself. Write this down before you start wallowing again and forget all about it. Try applying these words in your dealings with others, using their qualities as a tool to heal and enhance their lives, then see how such positive energy begins to spiral back to you. Start with the person who upset you today."

Was this my angel again, speaking to me through the sunlight and the tree? After all, we have already discussed how stress can be magnified by memories of similar events in the past. Was he here reminding me? Everything was suddenly fitting together, cooperating, working in harmony, I was connected again, I had been able to stop sinking into my own mud and the world looked brighter for it.

Instead, I sat down on the biggest of the protruding beech roots, took out my notebook and drew a clockwise spiral. I think the choice of direction was due to me being right-handed. There was no one around, so I voiced the words *praise-worthy-acceptance*, as I wrote them along the lines of the spiral, visualizing them circling through the entire wood towards the heart of the world beyond, as a gift. So many people could do with a bit of *praise-worthy-acceptance*. Wondering whether my words might merge with other resonant energies and spiral back to me, as the angel suggested, I allowed my imagination to create such an image, and in doing so, I felt like I was giving and receiving a blessing. I then repeated the exercise sending the same blessing to the person I felt had been unfairly critical earlier.

Harsh criticism meted out over a lengthy period, will more than likely cause the recipient to develop an equally destructive internal critic. Although we feel valued, whenever we receive compliments from others for our achievements, the external world gives us more positive feedback when we value ourselves. It is important to value and celebrate each success rather than wasting energy moaning about all the things that didn't work out. Changing this behavior, changes the internal landscape, which in time ought to manifest in value assigned by others since the internal and external worlds appear to be highly interactive.

Previous studies in Client Centered Counselling taught me how a counsellor's role was not to advise, but to facilitate change. Whilst different people need varying lengths of time to talk over the problems blocking their progress, they will also need to move on. There is a point where making the right intervention can empower another's understanding of a core issue, thus enabling them to negotiate or shift the obstacle. These are magical moments of possibility, which may bring about a change in the storyline. Remembering such knowledge, as well as the frequent favorable outcomes achieved using those skills in my former practice, caused a sudden realization, like dawn breaking bright across the horizon.

One notable benefit of getting older, is understanding how people who might have caused me pain in the more distant past are now either the same age as me, older still, or even dead in this present moment. And, since living my own life has radically changed me over the years, it is logical to assume that those who are still alive and with whom I have no further contact, might have also changed for better or for worse. Either way, I have concluded that there is nothing to be gained from getting mad about people who are now strangers. I have no wish to be a victim trapped in the past, by constantly digging up and replaying old worn-out material. Far better to forgive, send a blessing and move on as the path beckons. Issues with those who still play a part in my life can be dealt with in the energy of the moment, without reference to past hurts.

That day in the wood, I discovered how rituals using words work well for me, because I am a writer. The impression and visualization of spiraling energy are like a magic spell, a potent prayer, a personal mantra. I am also pleased to report the occurrence later in the day of a change in attitude towards me from my external critic. The magic had worked. However, I am quite sure that words need to be respected and used with care, as they are powerful tools, that can wound or heal. This is my reason for favoring a heart-centered path that creates no harm.

Transforming the words of habitual negative self-talk or unwarranted criticism might sometimes require the discipline of patient practice. This is not a new idea. Buddhism employs mantras and encourages right speech. Christians use words in prayer. I have been inspired to fit an old concept into a simple technique that suits my needs in the moment. I create a new story then tell it to others. I could even use the idea of a critic to create a character. An artist might see two different pictures, a musician two different tunes. A photographer I knew in London used to take pictures in such a way as to make familiar things look like something else. There are endless possibilities. Speaking words of genuine praise and blessing welcomes the angels and creates an atmosphere of cooperation. I often write short prayers, or poems to praise the natural world, which I can use both indoors and outside. I like to let the Creative Spirit and the angels know that they are welcome in my life.

I have written many a poem in Woodhall's woods, or sometimes resting on a bench under the spreading oak that stands just outside the fence surrounding the Catholic Church in the same village. Woodhall Spa is famous for housing RAF 617 Squadron better known as the *Dambusters* during World War Two, but as its name also suggests, it is today, very much a peaceful haven of trees. The inspiration I received to employ specific words to trigger the start of a self-healing process, was the first time I had ever noticed such a creative mind shift or really acknowledged an immediate power to change or rewrite my own story. I had indeed felt welcomed that day into a mythical realm of dryads or tree spirits. I had been praised and received a useful gift. To thank my angel, the beech and the sunlight for their wisdom and inspiration, for flowing with me in the Awen, I left a second rosebud in the moss growing around the base of that guardian tree.

Afterwards I felt free to walk on into the depths of the wood, where on this particularly hot day, rays of sunlight illuminated the darker places. It occurred to me that this was like the flashes of illumination that can sometimes come out of the forest of the unconscious mind. It can happen as gently as receiving the warmth of a friendly sunbeam, when I am living with awareness and intent, or it can hit the ground like a sudden bolt of lightning when I am not. There is strength to be discovered in the shadows that we fear, and treasures guarded by dragons that can sometimes be found in the darkest caves, revealed by a single flash of light.

To appreciate the light, we are often required to accept the fact that our lives have a corresponding shadow side. By sorting out the problems in the inner forest, cutting away the dead branches, allowing light to trickle into the symbolic woodland of our daily lives, we affect our understanding, thus paving the way for growth and change.

However, as a word of caution, I would hesitate to recommend too much introspection or over analysis since that might cause isolation, loss of energy, enjoyment and spontaneity. I can see no reason to go looking for trouble when life's path is smooth. Acknowledging and accepting obstacles whenever they arise from the parts of ourselves we do not like, instead of running away and avoiding life, is what I am getting at here. I would compare my own experience of allowing a strong emotion to emerge without acting it out, to walking through a forcefield instead of edging around it. There is always a still point at the center of a cyclone from which to observe and gain insight into the swirling spirals of debris. When I emerge from the experience, I find I can name the energy I had previously feared. Applying this wisdom, enables the discovery of hidden strengths, contained within the repressed material, thus releasing blockages that inhibit the flow of life.

Being a writer, I have made a personal decision to use words to facilitate my notion of alchemy, to symbolically transform my base metal into gold, to discover the light of wisdom from difficult life experience. Prompted by personal circumstances, memories of my formative years in the mining community of my great-grandfather, grandfather and father, I sometimes use the image of turning coal into diamonds, because it has some relevance to my own history.

My paternal great-grandfather was an Irish immigrant from a farming background, who came to seek his fortune in England, at a time when there was no work available in his homeland. He passed on a wonderful inheritance in the form of a singing talent, to my grandfather, who passed it on to my father, who then passed it on to me and my brother. My father, who sang classical songs around the working men's clubs in his spare time, had a wonderful tenor voice. In my own leisure time, I once enjoyed being a folk singer, a lead singer in an amateur rock band, an alto in two amateur operatic companies, which also involved acting, and finally joining in a concert party with four other singers. Today, my voice manifests as poetry, but when I'm prepared to stand up and sing from time to time, I find myself in a more mature place of depth and substance, a soul place.

I have been working steadily for years at turning the coal into diamonds, slowly bringing the harsher life, the darkness of the mines that once shaped the existence of my close ancestors, my immediate family and myself back into the light. I have found peace and inspiration in nature for as long as I can remember.

Today, I am acknowledging the threshold places, where the language of angels is easier to hear. I am listening to creative wisdom, the intelligence hidden everywhere in our beautiful planet, the endless sky and the vastness of a starlit universe.

From now on, I intend to pause at the entrance to woodland, and be mindful of the stream of thoughts flowing through my mind before crossing its threshold. I like to lean against any tree I feel drawn to, and I carry around a pocket guide to identify the ones I don't recognize. If I am troubled, I try to acknowledge and give time, allowing myself to feel emotions generated by the problem that is stealing my light, before I attempt to seek and merge its opposite. I accept that difficult times are part of life's experience. I have never heard of anyone who has had a totally trouble-free life. It is, however, possible to discover a balance, to develop a greater self-acceptance, with greater compassion for our wounded shadows. When we can do this and forgive ourselves, we find tolerance for the failings of our fellow humans in our own growing self-esteem.

I look at the sea through my balcony door, I take a few conscious breaths and allow feelings or images to flow into my imagination from the other side. It's all there, within and without, whenever I become aware that I am neither separated from this planet nor from the rest of the universe. I see that refusing responsibility for taking care of our own planet points to a lack of care or reverence for our very existence.

I believe when my father and mother met a small crack appeared in the dark spell cast by the mines. My mother also came from a farming background, forming a connection to the land again for my father. Even so, my mother's life in a mining community was fraught with difficulty. She was never able to feel completely at ease within its tough social structure and drinking culture. At the time of my birth, my parents lived with my maternal grandparents on their smallholding and my father worked in the bottle store of a local brewery. When I was four years old, my father moved us in with his parents, and from there, he started work with the National Coal Board, because it would offer us a house on a new estate about to be built in the next village. The mine had taken him. He went underground for us to have our own home and enough money to live on as an independent family.

The crack had repaired itself, the spell had taken hold again, causing emotional and social problems, until some twenty years later, when he graduated from an in-service City and Guilds course that gave him the qualifications to change from being a coal face worker to mine ventilation officer, respected by his colleagues. He had left school at fourteen, and until he passed those exams, none of us ever realized just how good he was at mathematics. He became an office worker with a couple of short trips down the mine shaft each day, to keep a check on the gas levels. Working on the surface was not only right for him it was right for all of us. Both his mood and his attitude to family improved. Further change happened when the coal ran out. My father was offered early redundancy and was thus able to retire a little earlier than he would have done otherwise. He took up woodwork and made beautiful toys for his grandchildren. The creativity had returned in a different form and the dark spell was shattered forever.

That former mining landscape has vanished without a trace and there is little evidence that it ever existed under all the spreading greenery. Once again, nature has taken possession of her kingdom. My brother and I were both state grammar school educated, so he never had to follow the men into those dank dark tunnels. He moved to rural Lincolnshire where he lives to this day, playing his guitar and singing in his spare time. My parents followed him there when my father became ill, a year before he died. At the time of writing, my mother is still alive, moving close to that final threshold. At the end of her days, she is happy in a rural community where she feels at home again.

She has come full circle. For myself, I will carry on along my way, crossing whatever thresholds appear to me, as well as continuing to practice word magic and alchemy as appropriate.

Practice

At those times you feel overwhelmed or emotional in relationships, seek solace and clarity from the natural world, wherever possible, weather permitting.

Trees, with their strong connection to earth through their root networks and to the sky through their branches, are strong companions to lean on in times of difficulty. They help us to hear our own negative self-talk and then to create a new focus. Ever since I was a child, I have experienced a strong feeling of safety among trees.

Try getting to know trees, by using a pocket guide to identify them.

Choose a tree that you feel particularly drawn to and make friends with it, by resting your back against its trunk either sitting on the ground or standing. See if you can tune into its life force through your spine or by putting your hands against the bark.

Now let the issue you are dealing with flow through your mind, as you tune into the tree, then try to detach from it and let your mind go as silent as possible. Notice any feelings, images or impressions that come to you through your connection to the tree. Attempt to change the energy you are creating by rewriting the personal story that keeps running through your mind. If you can do this, how will you express it? I use words, but you can use any medium you like working with. Try giving the blessing you need to someone who needs the same reassurance.

Don't worry if you don't succeed at first, as you might need to spend more time acknowledging and being with your own feelings. However, if you can, do try to make the effort to spend more time with trees, until you begin to feel rooted, supported and in tune with the language of angels, as it resonates through woodland.

Chapter Seven

Through the Senses

Storyteller

I am a storyteller a dream maker
all my tales are a rich woven cloth
of mystical thread I spin from gold
with dancing feet in the music of earth
I will sing you her life song of passion
as my fingers draw down a web of stars
to light her chalice the sky reflecting
a deep cauldron of plenty overflowing
this potion, of peace and magic growing
bright flowers blooming colour scented.
Iona Jenkins

I connect to inspiration through my senses, from which I develop an awareness of my place within my surroundings and the influence they have on me as a creative being.

Our early ancestors would have used their senses both fully and spontaneously like any other creature because survival would have depended upon their ability to do so. Today, however, in our modern technological world, we can order goods and services in seconds on a mobile phone. We are now consumers instead of hunters and gatherers, we have many creature comforts, but alas, we are also a people with increasing mental health and social problems.

So why are we not satisfied? Why does happiness elude so many? In losing our connection to the Divine Feminine, we have gradually been losing our connection to the planet which sustains us, which is why we are polluting our environment. We believe that we are separate, important, far above the rest of creation. In creating far too many boundaries, we avoid the oneness of our true reality, and we are lonely as a result. We could learn much from ethnic civilizations, living in communities with a powerful link to the natural world and a great respect for the land that nourishes them.

Many years ago, on a trip to the USA, I spent a few days in a spa in Arizona, before making my way north through Phoenix to Sedona, Flagstaff and finally on to the Grand Canyon. I had often felt drawn to that corner of the world with its Native American history, but as this was my first visit, I was open to exploration, and I wasn't disappointed with anything I found there. I was soon bowled over by the climate and the desert landscape dotted with cacti. It was August and even with temperatures soaring into heat such as I had never experienced, the air was so dry that I felt very little discomfort. I followed instructions to use sunblock, to wear socks and boots with shorts, not to forget my hat and to always carry a bottle of water. I stuck to the trails whenever I went out and stayed indoors, or in the shade during the middle part of the day.

On my first morning at the spa, I joined in the aerobic benefits of an early morning group walk. This activity was meant to kick-start a day of physical activity in the air-conditioned gym, a dip in the pool and a choice of therapies or classes. The walk certainly connected me to the landscape, but I wanted something more than just the exercise since I had never been surrounded by desert before. I needed to move more slowly outside, but the fast pace set by the trainer left me little time to take it all in, to feel the effect of this strange new environment on my entire being. I wanted to experience the quality of the light, to take a closer look at the cacti, the jackrabbits, the desert rats, the spiders, birds, butterflies and anything else that might be hanging around.

I carried on with those early morning aerobics for the sake of my body, but to exercise my soul, I also signed up for a walking meditation class that would enable me to move slowly through the same terrain, with the intention of really using all my senses.

The teacher, a laid-back individual with a French accent, led our small group out on to the desert trail. We paused frequently for reflection, as he talked us into feeling our connection to the land and the cloudless electric blue sky with its constant searing sun.

Next, he suggested thinking of this landscape as our home, our kingdom, feeling our connection to it. "You and the land belong to each other," he said, "imagine being in your kingdom. Observe the landscape, feel its influence, smell its scents, listen to its sounds and taste the air."

There was silence, as our teacher left us enough space to become one with the land. I soon realized he was asking me to do exactly what I had done automatically as a child, out there with my dog in the woods and fields around my Yorkshire home in England, so many years ago.

Back then, my kingdom had always offered me a benevolent safe place, especially when times were tough at home or in school. I knew where to find every wildflower in every season, the best elderberries, blackberries, wild garlic and birds' nests. I had a stream full of sticklebacks, frogspawn, or tadpoles, with moorhens swimming and wading or walking flat-footed along the bank on strange, webbed feet that looked almost alien.

There were groves with acorns, cones, beechnuts and chestnuts in autumn. There were suitable trees for climbing in any season and bush dens to hide in. Here was my magical kingdom, all contained within a two-mile radius of the British Coal Board estate, where I grew up. My memory, still vibrant and rich with such images, can always project this familiar landscape on to the screen of my imagination in the colors of every season, as bright and lush as any oil painting.

At last, enchanted by my new desert landscape, I was able to let those images of fertile green Yorkshire fade into the sunlight, to embrace the dry hues of Arizona and begin to create a new kingdom there. The teacher was speaking again, continuing with a guided meditation on a journey through the five senses, allowing us to experience each one of them in turn.

I have vivid memories of the powerful afternoon heat, penetrating my body right through to my bones, but without causing sweat, because of the total lack of humidity. The only water at that point in the walk, was contained in a bottle attached to my belt. It wasn't cool water, but its liquidity and taste offered a complete contrast to the air, parched and dry as the cracked earth below it. The sky, vast and cloudless, with a sun too bright to contemplate, stretched away in azure splendor, dominating the brittle desert soil, with no promise of a rainstorm any time that day.

The ground on which I walked, was crumbling into dust with no green scent. The cacti stood like prickly survivors, water storing for desert inhabitants, housing woodpeckers in a barren terrain where trees refuse to grow. I was alert, hoping for a glimpse of a rattlesnake or coyote, but unlike me, they would never have ventured out before the sun went down, and even then, they would have stayed away from any human trails.

Re-entering the cultivated landscape inside the spa complex, we passed a few jackrabbits, one or two scurrying desert rats, a single tarantula and even a roadrunner, which I noted bore no resemblance at all to the cartoon character, since it was brown and white speckled, about the size of a wood pigeon.

The walk ended in a desert-style cactus garden, bright with butterflies, flowers, and a man-made water feature. We had found our oasis. I was aware of cool droplets, splashing from the running fountain, adding refreshment to the habitual taste of dry air and the feeling of hot fiery earth. All four elements were as much present here as they had been in my British kingdom, only arranged in a very different way, like changing the pattern in a kaleidoscope. Fire and dry earth, startling, beautiful, stirring to the senses, it was a kingdom that had shaped the lives of Native American tribes in this area, who in their understanding of the landscape, had lived in harmony with it. Like all wild places, this desert kingdom has always demanded respect and cooperation from any human who values their own safety.

Following a second meditation using each of the senses in turn, our teacher suggested that we attempt to employ all five of them together. My first thought was that this would be impossible, but nevertheless, I was up for a challenge. I decided to begin with sight, my strongest sense, and then to try layering each of the others on top of it in rapid sequence. I found it difficult to hold on to my sense of sight, as I moved my attention to sound, then touch, then scent, then taste. I must have tried the experiment about ten times, until finally, for a split second, my awareness and the world seemed to expand into a flash of momentary brilliance. Of course, I couldn't keep hold of this consciousness, this state of expansion that I had touched but briefly. My two stronger senses of sight and feeling immediately became dominant again.

Maybe our human brains are not developed enough at this stage in evolution, to cope with such an expansion of perception for more than that split second. Perhaps it would be so mind-blowing that we wouldn't be able to handle an inrush of so much sensory information. I am certain that we have a way to go yet on that score. The way our senses operate, suits the way we are right now, but even so, with that one simple exercise, I had glimpsed the possibility of a sixth sense that could allow us to take in and understand more information in a safe way. I think that Native American shamans might have figured that out a long time before I ever turned up on their land.

I concluded that learning to use my senses in a more effective way, could afford me a greater connection to both my immediate environment and maybe even the whole of this wonderful creation we live in. I didn't think about it then, but today, I believe that my mind and heart had consciously begun to open to the language of angels, to Awen, that infinite flowing stream of inspiration, which had so often flooded my consciousness to make me creative, long before I ever discovered Italy or was able to put a name to it.

Traveling north towards the Grand Canyon, I spent a few days in Sedona, exploring some magnificent red rock formations sacred to Native American culture. Contemplating the natural structure of Cathedral Rock, my mind's eye picked up an impression of Celtic knotwork patterns superimposed upon its surface like a vast tapestry. It was as though I was seeing a connection not only between the Native American and Celtic cultures, but also between two very different lands thousands of miles apart. Celtic knotwork curves and intertwines without breaks in the pattern. Everything is linked in an energetic flow.

The angels were talking to me, showing me the Celtic world of my own ancestors in a faraway green misty landscape. New awareness was awakening from bonding with this fiery red earth place. The smooth flowing lines of knotwork in Celtic art suggest to me how the diverse peoples and lands of this planet are intertwined not only with each other, but with everything in the universe. In the same way, writing can connect me to art and music through the creation of patterns, color, resonance and harmony in words.

Most days, back home, I go for a walk around my more immediate environment, pausing to take in the landscape, as it changes through the seasons, visiting favorite trees and sitting in special places. I also watch the birds, the trees on the cliff top, the sea, the sky, the horizon, and the shoreline from the balcony of my apartment, pausing regularly to tune in through each of my senses, to the temperature, the feel and taste of the air, the scent of wet greenery and brown earth after the rain, the perfumes of flowers, all the changing colors and light, as the wheel of the year turns. I am becoming resonant with the moon phases, the brightness of the stars on a frosty night and the exquisite peace in the silence created by a blanket of snow.

Using my senses, I also notice how some activities and situations give me a noticeable boost in energy, whilst others feel draining. Developing this awareness, helps us to maintain the energy we need to live effectively. It's easy to miss out on all that is life enhancing, if we allow ourselves to be addicted to the stuff that wipes us out. This could be something as simple as a certain food or as complicated as a toxic relationship.

My angel connection always feels stronger when the moon shines bright on the ocean outside my window. I can find it among trees, when sunlight dapples through branches and breezes stir their leaves into a symphony. It also exists under a star-strewn sky or a garden alive with color. Inspiration can wash over me in a great wave at any time.

Most of us are gifted with five senses through which to experience the wonder of our existence in this beautiful world. Should one sense be impaired or lost, then one or more of the others will usually increase to compensate. To become aware, we need to pause, instead of acting like tourists, who are merely passing through, taking a few pictures and moving on. It is possible for us to create our kingdom anywhere, and if we create it in the heart, then the world outside becomes sacred as it reflects that existence. In this way, we might begin to realize we can feel at home wherever we are. We experience the joy of the moment, instead of dwelling on regrets about an unchangeable past or hurtling like runaway trains towards a future that does not yet exist.

My experience of connectivity in that vision of Celtic knotwork on the red rocks of Sedona, tells me how I can understand myself as an integral part of the whole. The whole benefits when individuals recognize, embrace and make some effort to understand their hidden parts, when they work on becoming whole, on developing love and tolerance for all life.

What if we do create everything with our minds as the Buddha and the angel have suggested? What if we are an intrinsic part of the creative force? What if the future is mutable and the thoughts we energize in the present do indeed bring it into being? If we were to stop our fighting and get together on that, could we not aspire to create a beautiful garden for all, rather than a self-centered spiritual and physical wasteland?

Anyone who attempts to do so becomes a part of the solution. Connecting to a Creative Spirit, relinquishing the need to control, in favor of a more enlightened cooperation, we glimpse the possibility and take responsibility, as we channel our energy into forging a better personal and global future from the *Now*. The senses can open the door into such a destination. We can light up the World.

Wherever you are, become the soul of that place.
Rumi

Practice

Often, when walking from A to B, we take little notice of the landscape. Instead, we focus on our destination and what we intend to do there, or we engage in constant mind chatter, rather than enjoying the journey itself.

Go out on a short walk in your local area for about half an hour, stopping frequently to focus on the world through one sense. For example, if you begin with sight, then really use your eyes to pick out landmarks, colors, textures, plants, trees, animals, birds, people, architecture, so that all this visual information starts to build a picture to replace the mental chatter. You will likely be surprised at all the things you never noticed before in an area that you thought you were familiar with. Make notes at the end of your walk.

In your own time, try the same walk, at roughly the same time of day, if possible, but focus on a different sense. Do this until you have used all five senses. Civilization has given us creature comforts, but it has also robbed us of much of the sensory ability that insured survival. It is amazing how different the air can smell or taste with changes of weather and season.

If you are already working creatively, notice whether having a sensory enhancement in your immediate environment has increased your inspiration. If you are not, ask yourself whether using your senses more efficiently links you to any kind of inspiration?

Take time to find out how your senses respond to different kinds of weather, different seasons, or the light at different times of day and what effect that has on you as a whole being.

Chapter Eight

Wisdom Walking

Alone

I celebrate the fact
that I am alone
I let go of wanting
to be with others
for that is not here
and that is not now.
Understanding this moment
I find my freedom
in the full experience
of this alone time
under the trees.
Iona Jenkins, Heartsong, 2016

When I first came to live in Wales, I became interested in the practice of mindfulness, and since then, I have tried to integrate mindful walking into my personal spiritual life, so that each small journey becomes as much of a moving meditation as walking a labyrinth. This practice of paying attention, instead of getting hooked up into a mass of internal chatter, is proving an excellent way of increasing my ability to tune into the environment. It builds upon the work I did in Arizona to train and refine my senses, to raise my awareness to another level. Intensifying my sensory experience, not only provides me with a heartfelt expression of artistic inspiration. It also lights up my mind and increases my understanding, which is why I like to call it Wisdom Walking. I now invite you to accompany me on such a walk into the woods.

I am spending Christmas in Lincolnshire with my husband

and family as usual. It is late morning on the day after the Winter solstice, when I decide to head off towards Woodhall Spa village to enjoy a solitary walk in the woods. It is the first sunshine after a lengthy period of heavy rain that has created a watercolor landscape, a canvas of faded greens, ochres, and soft browns under a misty blue sky lit with a pale buttery glow of sunlight.

A powerful scent of damp earth mixed with wood curls into my nostrils, as I take in a breath of air that tastes watery, almost drinkable, and quite unlike the salt flavor that lingers on my lips when I walk by the sea. I am wearing layers of clothes to keep in the heat, a waterproof jacket, boots and gloves, so that only the skin on my face tingles with winter cold.

Surprised at the volume of dried copper leaves still clinging thick to numerous beech hedges, I forget to consider my feet and almost walk into a huge puddle covering most of the path, where a few uneven paving stones form a dip in the pavement. I veer to the left, edging my way around it, realizing I must pay more attention to the ground, as the layers of leaf mold mixed with slippery mud could cause a serious fall and broken bones should I ignore them. This is a greater consideration for me now than it might have been even ten years ago. I make a mental note to include my feet in my experience and to be careful not to cut them off from the rest of my body, whether I am walking or sitting. This matters a lot, as they form my primary connection to the earth. My consciousness needs to inhabit my whole body, not just my head, so I will know whether I am in good health, what gives me pain, what is life enhancing and what is not. Like a tree, I need to be rooted if I want to set my sights on the stars, without falling over.

Before I even reach the wood, it appears to be sending out its wisdom. I continue, drawn by my connection to the trees. Some of them are now only clothed in their greyish brown bark, but the silver birches have retained their color and elegance even without leaves. Wispy sunlight glitters through the stark outlines of bare branches that stretch upwards like gnarled bones. Some are ivy cloaked in deepest green, whilst others are olive and moss tinted, but there is only one tree heavily laden with berries like ruby jewels, standing close to a lime-hued laurel bush. Here, a cock pheasant struts his stuff in gaudy feathers on the grass verge, only a short distance from the woodland. All this color, bright as Indian cushions, seems almost out of place, as though it ought to be included in an oil painting instead of a watercolor. It is an interesting effect of nature that makes a strong impression on my senses of sight and touch (feeling).

Moving on, I look skywards, where a great commotion is taking place, a caw cawing cacophony, deafening amidst a busy flock of black wing flapping activity. My focus drifts from sight to sound to include a noise that had previously only existed in the background. I listen, then refocus, to observe a rookery of five large nests, where a host of birds coming and going in their own sky-high world seem quite oblivious to any human beings pottering about on the ground below. It is a peaceful coexistence of two different species separated by the height of the tallest trees. Earth and sky in harmony. I wonder what they are talking about with all that noise in their tree-top territory.

I am obliged to walk along the narrow tarmac road now, following the boundary of the wood. There is far too much water and mud to ramble amongst the trees today. It will take days to dry out again. Even so, the knotted bare branches of old deciduous trees and the bluish evergreen of tall pines seem to reach out to me, as I acknowledge their presence and leave my usual dried rosebud. I may be road walking, but I am on the edge of a wood, a threshold place, where I always feel welcome and where the trees keep me company. The wood seems to be breathing, so I pause and attempt to tune in, to breathe in harmony with it. When I picture all those individual tree roots snaking their way through the soil in a vast underground network, I feel like I am almost being carried along the road, with my feet hooked into the system. The experience is soul nurturing and I know that I am safe, protected.

This is the way it was for me as a child, and now in my elder years I notice once more, that nothing has changed. It is I who lost the connection and forgot the trees during my working adult life, with all its hectic city living. It is strange then, how I can trace the beginning of my journey back to them, from the time I first began exploring the banks of the River Thames, and the parks and gardens of busy West London. I have returned for good now. I am theirs again and they are mine. All is well and as it should be at this time in my life. By using and refining my senses, I hear the angels speaking to me once more through the spirits of trees in the wood.

I acknowledge that I love this chilly winter season as much as I love the warm summer. The elements have been mixed into a particular potion, a different color scheme, a faded background palette but with sharp outlines and cooler temperatures. This year, however, there have been very few hard frosts, their ice crystals sparkling in moonlight. There is no winter snow yet and these higher temperatures have created downpours, floods with day after day of intermittent heavy showers.

As I reach the end of the lane, I turn left to walk back towards the main road where I can sit on a bench, or even better in the bookshop café with a cappuccino and a notebook to record all the sensory impressions from my walk. Sometimes these impressions are mixed into potions of creative wisdom through a poem, a simple two-liner or the beginning of an idea that might one day develop into a longer piece of prose or philosophy. As it turns out, today's magic potion has turned into this chapter.

This side of the wood is flooded and there is a puddle as big as a small pond. The roadside ditch, unable to cope with such a huge volume of water, has poured it out amongst the trees. The water evokes a wave of sadness, as our Mother Earth sighs and whispers her sorrow through the angels and spirits of the wood. The trees are telling me her tale and I am aware that we all need to listen. The angel voice resonates around my heart space.

"Use your art to help raise awareness, by inspiring others to awaken their creative heart wisdom and open new doors of possibility. Humanity has unbalanced the elements and so you must all begin to rewrite this story before your earth world becomes a water world. The polar ice caps are thinning with global warming. You have inherited this planet from your ancestors. You are custodians, responsible for helping to maintain and pass it on, so that many generations may follow and evolve in her care."

I listen and agree willingly to the angel's request, hoping and praying that January, after three washed-out months, might see a return to those bright frosty days. I would even welcome the arrival of a heavy snowfall, bringing with it a promise of change. And, since I have a deep sense that some sort of change is imminent, I make a resolution to keep my senses honed and open to the messages that flow into me from the natural world. I take three breaths and thank the wood for its teaching, before heading off to the bookshop for that welcome cup of coffee.

My attention is soon drawn skyward by a fluttering trio of small birds, a flash of blue and yellow. A weary wood pigeon sleeps silent, balancing on a high bare branch. There is a faint cool breeze, and the sun looks almost white now in the ice blue sky dotted with moving clouds of silver grey. I breathe the sharp earthy scent of winter as the air caresses my face. Something inside me is saying that it will rain again before the end of the day.

Practice

Now that you have become accustomed to really employing your senses more efficiently, you might like to try your own Wisdom Walk, in a location where you feel comfortable and safe, preferably away from busy roads to start with.

Feel free to pause any time you like to note down any ideas that might come to you during your walk. You can also find comfortable places to sit either during or at the end of your sensory stroll to mull over, describe or note key words to record whatever occurs to you, from enhancing your sensory relationship with the landscape.

Chapter Nine

Time and Place

I Know Not Where?

The dazzling sunrise amber red and gilded
bursting through a cloud of charcoal grey
to set me on fire with colour exploding
an untamed wind rushing in from the sea
where wild waves are distant roaring lions
beyond a sunlit path upon the water shining
a golden gate that leads to I know not where?
Iona Jenkins

In my imagination, the entrance to my creative heartland takes the form of a golden door or sometimes a golden gate. I have never visited the American city of San Francisco, though its Flower Power youth culture did have an influence on my thinking towards the end of the nineteen sixties. I remember how I had once looked at a picture of its Golden Gate Bridge and said to myself,

"One day I'm going to cross that bridge!"

As a matter of fact, although I have never quite got round to making that trip, I could still plan and enjoy a week away in San Francisco should I feel so inclined. However, a sudden insight tells me that I don't need to go there right now, since the idea of a golden gate bridge is in fact symbolic for me. The American City of San Francisco is named after Saint Francis, and I have already made that journey to the Italian town of Assisi, where he was born and died. I often experience threads of association that seem to link ideas, people and places within me whether or not I choose to take an actual physical journey.

This golden gate or door is an image that often appears in my mind's eye whenever I wake up early enough to watch the sun rising. At the time of writing this chapter, we are in the month of October, and this morning, I was up early with my phone, taking pictures of deep yellow, orange, red and charcoal autumn sky colors, as the rising sun dissolved the cloud, to cast its path of molten gold, like a shining bridge across the ocean. Here was my mystical Golden Gate Bridge, a sunrise door opening into this chapter, with a dawn chorus of feathered harmony and angel song. The Otherworld was wide-awake, pouring out a colorful stream of inspiration.

It is not only at sunrise, that I am so receptive, though that is the usual time for such golden gate visions. My soul also flows freely with Awen and angels at twilight, in bright moonlight, when the air is still and the sky is alive with stars, when the wind stirs the trees, or rays of sunlight dapple through leaf laden branches. Ideas can come at any hour of day or night, and the angel often turns up late when the moon shines bright above the sleeping world in Wales. During these special times of dawn and twilight, however, at the threshold between day and night, I am in tune with the Creative Spirit and ideas flow easily into poetry, prose or story.

Although I do not wake at dawn every day, I am sometimes pulled out of bed if the angels have something to say. Time and place, then, are important to the creative process, which does not always fit with either convention or human habits. This morning, the balcony outside my apartment was such a place and the sunrise was the right time.

I get a strong sense of time with the sun, from its rising to its setting. I am sometimes aware of how my body feels, or how strong or weak my concentration can be at different times of day. I also feel subtle differences in the air, the temperature, the earth scents, when the season is changing. Since I began doing the moonlight meditations and writing the angel conversations, I have been paying closer attention to the moon phases and their effect on me. If I am preoccupied with other things, then, this sensitivity is easily overridden, because unlike my ancestors I am not dependent on it for my survival. If I had sufficient skill to tune in through my senses all the time, I feel sure that life would flow with natural synchronicity.

My best time of day for drafting and editing my lines of handwritten inspiration into files on my computer is around 4pm, but sometimes later in summer. My concentration is better for this type of work when the sun is closer to the west and on its journey towards twilight. Creative activity varies from person to person, and we can all find our own productive zones. I always work at the same desk in the same room and having such a dedicated space also feels like an important part of the process. I like attractive paper notebooks and pens for jotting down a flow of words, because as tools, they suit my fingers better for working quickly with any burst of inspiration. Others might prefer a smartphone or iPad. There are no rules governing this and anyone can be more creative using their own sacred times, places and methods or rituals.

In my time, I have visited several places considered to be sacred, sites that have become well signposted, because many people have trodden their pilgrim paths both before and after me. These are places, where the curtain between the actual world and the Otherworld appears thinner. I think that my sense of the sacred has been increased by these excursions, because they have always left me with a feeling of creative presence, touching me deeply and following me home, building up over time, nourishing and inspiring, infusing my life with their influence.

I am speaking of sites such as Lindisfarne, Iona and the Scottish Isles, Glastonbury and Stonehenge in England, the Newgrange burial site and the Hill of Tara in the Boyne Valley of Ireland, then on into the mountains of Connemara and the light of the western shores beyond them. In Wales, I love Snowdonia in the north, then heading into the west, the Gower Peninsula, St. Bride's Bay and Saint Non's Well on the outskirts of St. David's, Pembrokeshire. In America, the Arizona desert, the red rocks of Sedona and then the Grand Canyon, where landscapes shape change in shadow and light, with the passage of clouds across the sky. In India, the Hindu Temples of Khajuraho, the stupa in Sarnath, where the Buddha is reputed to have preached his first sermon, the Himalayas, and the temples of Kathmandu in Nepal. In Italy the Vatican's Sistine Chapel, Assisi and Florence. These are only a few places of wonder on my own short list and there is a whole world out there to explore. I am not done yet, so I remain open, hoping to be awed, inspired or nurtured by a few more wondrous lands on our planet before my time comes to leave it. We must seek out and experience sites that work best for us, in the same way as we choose our friends.

A sense of the sacredness of our Earth and the Universe are influencing my path towards that golden door. I am discovering small, unknown, but none the less significant spots in my own area. I begin to link up the images, I see a gateway to the stars through the branches of a tall pine, I am often inspired to write angel conversation when a full moon shines bright over the sea and I can access the golden gate and its bridge from my own home at sunrise. As I continue to create, so my inner landscape becomes more and more infused with this inspirational light, this Awen that brightens the shadows, as I let my creations spill out into the world of form.

I have discovered that sacred places can also facilitate change, but not, of course, with the empathy of a person-centered counsellor. As some sites have very powerful energies that have built up over centuries, I think it is always wise to take good care when embarking on any kind of pilgrimage. Even though there may be inspiration that results in new bursts of creativity, the push to change needed to accommodate it, can sometimes be challenging. Like meditation and the inner world, there are places in the outer world that are best visited only when both mind and body are stable and well.

Two trips to India and one to Nepal and the Himalayas have taught me to be more cautious, by snapping me out of my complacency with bouts of acute physical illness, that not only took weeks to cure upon my return home, but also forced me to review several aspects of my life, to adjust and change accordingly. I have developed a great respect for the wildness and unpredictability of mountains since they stretch my consciousness towards the Universe. Even on the top of our own gentler Mount Snowdon with its tourist trains to the summit and well-worn paths for walking, I had an impression of a star shining in daylight sky above my head.

Some pilgrims make their way up Mount Kailash, the most sacred mountain in the Himalayas, but I know I am nowhere near physically strong enough to even think about doing that now, so I have become content to stick to more accessible places. It is necessary to develop an understanding of our own limits and to set ourselves appropriate boundaries. So far, I have been blessed with enough courage and energy to deal with the emotional fallout and physical pain that have entered my own life, even if at times, it felt like standing at the edge of a precipice. Although my experience tells me I will somehow always find a foothold, it does not necessarily take all the anxiety out of the equation. I have concluded that there is little point in looking for crosses to carry, when I can find ways to grow and create without doing so.

India and Nepal, two countries close together with very different atmospheres, have none the less left wonderful pictures stored forever in my memory. As well as numerous images of temples, tombs, palaces and people, I recall the stunning nature of these Eastern landscapes. In Nepal, sitting outside a hilltop restaurant with a viewing point, I breathed in the light of a New Year's Eve sunset, painting the Himalayan snow peaks in mystic metallic rose. In India, I marveled at the pure white marble of the Taj Mahal, inlaid with bright flowers crafted from semiprecious stones. Then, in the town of Varanasi, I sat in a rowing boat, floating my tea light on the Ganges at dawn, before watching the sun rise above the horizon like a huge orange and gold ball lighting both sky and water with new life and fire.

However, grateful for having experienced such wonders, I am also aware that the Himalayas belong to a more youthful time of my life, and as such, I have no yearning to make further outer world excursions in their direction. I can, however, use my stored images to visit them as internal landscapes in my imagination whenever I want to. Some people are more physically and mentally robust than others and as my own decision is based on my age and personal experience, I can only suggest that you use your own intuition and knowledge of personal safety parameters to guide you towards whatever sites may beckon you on.

A yoga teacher in London once advised me to work slowly, to only push the body as far as it was prepared to go in any one session, and then gradually, in its own time, capability would likely increase to achieve more. It is necessary to understand our own limits, to be gentle and respectful towards body and soul. Take good care, check out any new terrain before you go rushing into it. Connect by walking with respect, asking for nourishment, guidance and safe passage, and by leaving a gift to say thank you.

My experiences in the Italian town of Assisi were joyful and life enhancing rather than therapeutic, sending me home full of inspiration and creative energy. I found myself powerfully connected not only to the town, but to the landscape outside its walls.

The sunshine of early June was soft like sunflower petals. This was an experience of a gentle allowing and creative solar energy, rather than the patriarchal and ruling masculine sun deity I had come to expect. I could sense a presence, the golden heart of a Creative Spirit in the groves of olive trees, I could smell it in the scent of olive oil, taste it in regional Italian food accompanied by a glass of local wine enjoyed on the outdoor verandas of small trattorias. I could feel it in the warm sun-kissed stones of ancient buildings, I could hear it in the lively interactions of local people, and once again I experienced that feeling of being at home.

In the Piazza del Commune, I discovered the frontage and pillars of a temple to the ancient Roman goddess Minerva built in the first century BCE. Behind this façade, the church of Santa Maria sopra Minerva was built in 1539 and then renovated further in Baroque style during the 17th century. The statue of the Virgin Mary crowned in electric light stars dominates the Altar, looking modern and typically Catholic. Assisi is yet another place where the veil separating the outer and inner worlds feels thin. The land is warmed by that soft sunflower sun, and I sense the enduring presence of a Goddess, a strong sacred feminine that predates both temple and church.

And this floral sun did not burn, it warmed me into contentment, releasing a burst of writing inspiration. I found myself wondering whether Francesco Bernardone (St. Francis of Assisi, 1183-1226) had also experienced something along these lines, only much more intense, because he had a great creative spiritual destiny to follow, when he left his wealthy family and the town's oppressive religious regime, to live as a poor monk. First, he set about renovating a small, ruined church at San Damiano, which lies on a hillside just outside the city walls. Here, he created a new kind of community, based on a nature inspired, inclusive Christianity, where all could share in a simple, nurturing and healing spirituality, regardless of wealth or status. In his rebellion against social injustice, he appears to have dived deeply into the essence of Christ's teachings, bringing back the energy of his Divine Mother to care for the children of this new congregation.

Many young people chose to follow his example, though he was berated and cast out by the local powerful and wealthy hierarchy. He walked to Rome to ask the Pope what he had done wrong. The Pope, shamed by such simple love and dedication, wholeheartedly gave his blessing to Francis's work. The life of this saint shows how spirituality can sometimes be at odds with organized religion, especially where there might be a need for change. But undaunted, Francis followed his heart and his path proved true. He not only built a community he also created a story, a legend, that has lived on, to inspire so many people down the centuries, myself included.

Francis is also renowned for his great connection to the whole of nature, spending time in prayer and spiritual contemplation in a cave on the hillside. Amongst his writing are canticles to the sun and to the creatures. He also spoke of the sun and moon as his brother and sister. The mystic was a visionary, a writer, a restorer of churches, an inspirer, a healer, as well as a campaigner for social equality and spiritual reform, who both listened and responded to his language of angels.

> *The greatest mystics of the middle-ages were among the birthers of our contemporary Western Languages. Each was at the heart of a battle for a new language in order to name a new experience. Each was engaged in what we might call the search for 'new wineskins.' Francis of Assisi and Dante were launchers of the Italian language. Francis's Canticle to the Sun has long been considered one of the finest poems in the Italian language.*
> **Matthew Fox, *The Coming of the Cosmic Christ*, p. 58, HarperOne (Harper Collins 1988)**

The Hermitage of Eremo Delle Carceri, built over Francis's meditation cave, is located about four kilometers east of Assisi, on the wooded slopes of Mount Subasio. Here I discovered a peaceful sanctuary, where the breeze whispers through the leaves and the sun sends strands of golden light rippling down into forest shade. The stars seen by Francis in the night sky must have been spectacular back then, and it's likely they still are.

The Saint's most renowned supporter was a woman called Chiara Offreduccio (St. Clare, 1193-1253). They are depicted as great friends and spiritual companions. Accredited with healing ability and miracles herself, she was younger and outlived Francis by about seventeen years. Although she is less famous outside Assisi, the importance of Clare should not be overlooked. Their relationship was deemed to be of a purely spiritual nature, and she provided a powerful feminine energy in the movement at that time. Francis worked with a band of brother monks and Clare founded an Order of nuns. The Franciscans and the Poor Clare Orders are very much alive today. There are many pictures of the two saints together, and that feels both balanced and right to me.

I continued my exploration of Assisi with a view to trying to get in tune with the spirit of Francis and Clare, by connecting to the surrounding countryside and meditating in the simple Church of San Damiano in preference to the more elaborate, often crowded Basilica. I did, however, visit the Basilica twice for an evening meditation at the Saint's tomb, towards the end of my stay. In daylight, I chose San Damiano for its rustic simplicity and for the fact that Francis first discovered his life's mission, sitting in front of its old Byzantine cross, which fortunately had remained intact even after the church became derelict.

I strolled through Assisi's ancient narrow streets, pausing to buy a book of Francis's writing, as well as two slim, illustrated paperbacks on the lives and times of each of the saints. I dipped into the beauty of the Saint's words, though in English translation, but as my intuitive mind was beginning to paint its own picture, I waited until the end of our trip before turning a single page of the life story booklets to fill in all the historical details.

My husband's purchase was a beautiful pottery wall plaque, a yellow smiling sun face on a blue background. The image has a feminine softness, as though it had been brushed by the hand of the Goddess. There are many such beautiful sun faces to be found in artisan pottery shops throughout Italy. It seems to me that Francis in his sensitivity had found the wisdom and love in his heart to work positively with a dynamic feminine wisdom, added to a gentle, inclusive, and creative masculine will to be of service that reflected the true message of the Christ he followed. His ability to open to love and the landscape around him, made him both a great catalyst for change and a creator of legends. There is little wonder that I can feel an increase in life force, when I stand on my balcony and breathe in the sunrise.

In the green Irish mountains of Connemara, my soul mingled easily with the soul of Ireland, and I felt completely at home. I had that same experience on the Scottish island of Iona, floating between two worlds in the Atlantic mists. I had such a powerful connection, to this tiny island, it was as though the land was calling me by her own name, accepting me as a part of her. I decided to increase my therapeutic skills by studying hypnotherapy after visiting Iona, where one day, watching the sun setting huge and fiery red in the west, stirred an idea about healing with words. As that inspiration grew, I adopted Iona as my own creative name. Today, I sometimes sense a healing energy of words flowing through certain aspects of my writing. A single sunset on a sacred Scottish isle, had communicated a sense of joy, nurture and belonging too amazing to describe. We can have so much of what is right for us whenever we stop trying to control, when we open ourselves to the generosity of the wonderful creation all around us, trust in our lives and discover that we really are not alone.

Within the sacred ancestral stones of Stonehenge, I received an impression of starlight even in the afternoon. I enjoyed the deepest peace sitting by Chalice Well, in the first high wind of autumn, as it whooshed and sighed so loud through the yew branches. The day after, working for the first time ever with a group of Druids, about thirty people I had never met before, I found my poetic/bardic voice on a weekend workshop in Glastonbury. The participants had been divided into four small teams, each working on a short presentation related to one of the seasons that would form a quarter part of a whole group ceremony.

As my group settled into the task, of presenting the winter season, it was interesting to embrace the resonance and empathy we found together, in joining our voices to sing the Awen. Without any prompting, everyone was able to slide easily into a part of the ritual that would enable them to contribute their personal talents, without taking either time or space away from anyone else. It was a real team effort, as the five separate creative energies of our group blended and supported each other in an effective finished product that, in its turn, flowed easily into the whole event.

The ingredient I added into the mix was a poem I had penned on the spot in ten minutes. I had never recited any of my poems in such a way before, so it was with joy and surprise I first heard the power, tone and expression contained within my own voice, resonating with the steady beat another member of my group was creating on a drum decorated with rainbow ribbons. I can only describe it as taking my turn in the center, adding my energy into the mix. In ten spoken lines, I experienced the performance ability of the bard/poet/storyteller, an ability to act out the words using my voice and my body. What's more, I was able to witness the positive effect that my acting and reciting that poem had on several people, as well as feeling the positive energy I received from watching and listening to the efforts of others. Four groups working separately achieved resonance and harmony in making up the whole. One of our workshop leaders later commented on the finding of my voice. I had at last realized the confidence to give that gift, without the slightest hint of anxiety and to understand that it had been well received. I had both accepted and given respect.

All four seasonal contributions to the ceremony were a joy, and I can see now, how the other members of my small team had effectively lifted me over a hurdle, with their acceptance of all that I was, in allowing me the space and freedom to remember my voice and use it to express myself in the ceremony. I have from time to time lived or worked in places where my voice has not been appreciated, where I might also have backed down, because I couldn't summon enough courage in the moment, to stop the egos and ambitions of others from silencing me. Here, however, no one had wanted to shut me up, and for that, I give my heartfelt thanks to everyone involved in that event for their respect. It was a healing, a rare piece of Glastonbury magic to be sure.

The drama of speaking my poetry in a team effort, felt like birth, a new beginning, and who knows, I may yet in the future find suitable opportunities for opening doors into the imagination of an audience with my poems and stories like a true bard, by sometimes using the spoken word as a more theatrical alternative to the written one.

I will continue to enjoy discovering sacred places wherever I may travel, whether at home or abroad, and on each local walk, varying the paths I take, allowing time and space for the angels of place to speak to me through the landscape with its plant life and its creatures. As always, I continue in my aspiration to reflect the peace, light and inspiration out into the world from the land that exists beyond a golden gate when the sun rises.

Practice

Pay more attention to your body, so that you begin to discover the times of day or night when you feel most energized. Where and when do you prefer to work on creative projects? What energizes or relaxes you in terms of scents, colors, music etc. Examine your methods and tailor them as far as you can to suit your physical, mental and emotional well-being.

Make a short list of the landscapes that have really touched your heart. Which ones really stand out and why? How do you feel connected to these places? It may be that one or more of these sites has influenced your creativity in the past and that they can still do so in the present. Now, think about places you feel drawn to but have never visited. You might like to consider planning a trip if you have the time, resources and capacity to do so.

By now, you may also have discovered more than one inspirational site close to home, where you can continue to train your senses and build up your stream of inspiration. When you feel ready, try creating something, however small, in honor of one of them.

Chapter Ten

Raven Moon

Into The Mystery

A Solitary black raven
balancing in a sycamore
swaying shadow silhouette
on a swirling back drop
of autumnal misting sky
and water grey sea wash
spreading ragged edge wings
she rises, takes off, then glides
flying deep into the mystery.
Iona Jenkins

I have discovered that my consciousness spans two worlds. First and foremost, there is the solid outer world of form relating to the conscious mind and its intellect, our everyday reality. Then there is the inner world of dreams, myths and legends, the realm of unconscious mind and imagination. Within and without, both worlds are alive with wondrous things to fill my poems and stories. In the outer world, they already have form, but in the inner world, they remain in a state of possibility.

Meditations and daydreams sometimes take me on quests for hidden treasures through inner landscapes. On such a journey I might encounter obstacles, tricksters, and challengers, before I can illuminate those treasures with a magic lantern of moonlight and eventually give them form in the world outside. Sometimes a guide might appear, when the time is right, and today, I feel inclined to fly with a raven. It is now Monday 28th October, and Halloween or All Souls, is on Thursday of this week. This ancient Celtic festival of Samhain is not really a time to be frightened by ghouls and vampires, it is rather a time when we remember and honor the Ancestors. This is when we can let go of the ghosts of the past and unproductive ways of thinking, before the first of November, which traditionally used to mark the beginning of the Celtic New Year.

I acknowledge the raven as a wise bird of the mysteries, for the creature has that look about it, as though it could glide through the night into forgotten corners of the unconscious mind, where untold magic and jewels lie hidden. Black as midnight, she is a sleek Amazon amongst birds with her impressive wingspan, sparkling eye, and solid curved beak, which gives her an ancient appearance. Her voice is raucous, strident like a wake-up call, as she struts bossily across the grass or sails above cliffs, carried on sea winds, fearless and sure of herself in all weathers.

This morning, she landed for a few seconds, speaking with a crack-cracking sound, as though she was laughing and shouting,

"Time to get moving!"

Then all at once, she rose into the air in pursuit of a passing magpie and was gone before I had chance to think.

I continued to notice her at different times of day, perched upon the swaying branch of a tree. Several times she flew past my window until I went for my notebook and penned a poem to celebrate her. At twilight, she vanished into the mist.

That twilit hour has now passed and the trees on the edge of the cliff are waving shadows in a wild night. I light my candle lantern to meditate though I am obliged to keep the door shut, because this night is lashing stormy under a waning moon crescent. Tomorrow the darkness takes over, as the new moon returns and will not begin her first waxing phase until the day after Halloween. I snuggle under my blanket in the warmth of flickering candlelight, tuning in to the untamed sound of a wild wind whipping up the sea. At three hours past high tide, my eyes begin to close, but not with sleep for something is hovering on the edge of my consciousness. I remember the raven and her flight into the mystery.

Tonight, there is no moonlight path for my angel to walk upon, though I sense his presence with the waning crescent hanging thin, a mere sliver of light falling into the inky black space behind the clouds.

"I am your calm on a stormy night, strong as an oak mast, when you fear that the turbulence of an emotional sea might overwhelm you."

At last, I have a full impression of my angel all bright pearly light that's flecked with splashes of pale colors above the noisy surging sea. In his right hand, he carries a lantern that sheds bright pools of moonlight about his feet.

"Why the lantern?" I ask.

"The light that the waning moon had left behind, is no longer visible, but I have captured it in this lantern so you may see your way clearly through any hidden obstacles awaiting you in the darker corners of your inner forest," the angel says, looking like he means business. "When you shine moonlight on such obstacles, you start to see them in their true perspective. It is as easy as flipping a coin so that treasure appears on the other side of shadow. Are you ready?" he asks holding out a hand to me.

"Thanks for that," I say feeling just a little uncertain. "I can't go out tonight, it's far too stormy, so I suppose this is a good time to venture in. I never want to go looking for problems, but I think you are neither about to let me off the hook nor allow me to avoid what you seem to want me to find. I would obviously prefer to find something beautiful, a wonderful treasure that offers no hassle."

"You and everyone else," he laughs, "but this particular inner journey has need of my lantern and in the next few days after we've done our moonlighting, then you will feel empowered from facing your challenge. Not only that, I think you may also find a new treasure, a strength hidden within an instinct or emotion, you did not want to face, so there may be something beautiful after all."

"Challenges are treasures in disguise then? They have that potential if I have the courage. Right?"

"Mm not bad." He smiles warmly, holding up his lantern of moonlight. "Are you coming with me or not?"

"Okay, you win."

I relax and follow him in my imagination, as he opens a door in the storm and walks right through it. The air is still on the other side, the landscape green and the sky summer blue. There is a bearded man sitting at a stone table and I realize that I am seeing a picture from a set of divination cards I own. It is *The Arthurian Tarot* by John and Caitlin Mathews, and this image is very like the first card of the major arcana which is called the Magician or Merlin in this pack. I find myself in a Celtic landscape, a mythical Britain known as Clas Myrddin or Merlin's Enclosure.

The unexpected vision of Merlin is an indication I am entering a period of new energy and creativity. The Magician acts as mediator between the inner and outer landscapes, facilitating visions and feelings from the dreams of intuitive mind, so they may manifest in the world of form through the artist's creative skill. With an accurate interpretation of symbolic angel language, my magician would speak the words of making from the beauty of a poetic heart, allowing Creative Spirit to flow through him into appropriate art forms.

Then, considering the legendary power of magicians, I am reminded of *The Sorcerer's Apprentice*, a tale that speaks of patience, learning wisdom, exercising caution, and showing respect.

"I'm a mere apprentice," I say to the angel. "I don't always get it and I mess up frequently. But why are you showing me this?"

"First for you to understand what you are doing," he explains. "Secondly, I know that you have a few packs of divination cards and that I often show you pictures from them when you are trying to work something out, even if you don't ask. You might like to consider asking more often instead of struggling. The age of martyrdom is over for you and spiritual living in this world is going in a new direction. Evolution and all that."

"I do get help by seeing card images sometimes," I answer, "but I never associated it with you."

"And are the answers you get from those images connected to what you are engaged in or trying to work out?" he asks.

"Always."

"Well then," he adds, "that's one way to find a door in the dark or in a storm, isn't it? I turn up with my lantern of moonlight and illuminate your mind with a picture, because sight happens to be your strongest inner sense. The moon is often associated with the intuitive mind. The light shows up in symbols, to point you towards whatever you need to be aware of."

"So, is Merlin a symbol then?"

"Merlin represents different things to different people, but he is definitely an archetypal magician, right there in your unconscious mind, mediating between your inner and outer worlds and providing creative impulse. You grew up with the Arthurian legends, did you not?"

"Yes, and I've always loved them," I say, remembering.

"And they speak to you through your personal relationship with the land. By the way, anyone can tune into them even if they come here from a different part of the world."

"Is that how I tapped into native America?" I ask, remembering that powerful experience again. "And Sedona in Northern Arizona is steeped in Native American history and legend. I had booked a Jeep tour to some of the old power spots and the journey began not far from my lodgings, right where the Apache nation is reputed to have come to earth.

Afterwards the tour guide took us to a Native American Medicine wheel, constructed from stones on the top of a hill. It looked exactly like the shape of a round Celtic cross in a circle, which has no base and is sometimes also referred to as a cross of harmony, with four equal sides. This symbol has obviously been used by the Ancestors of different cultures and is way older than Christianity.

Finally, we visited the major rock formations, all named according to whatever their shape suggested. Our group formed a circle on the ground below Cathedral Rock, where the tour guide invited each one of us to take a card from her divination pack of animal Medicine Cards. I remember drawing a card, which had an image of a hawk, the messenger. I looked up at Cathedral Rock and once again had an impression in my mind's eye, of Celtic knotwork patterned across the entire rock face."

"So, tell me what you learned from your messenger hawk," the angel says looking interested.

"That I might find the same wisdom back in Great Britain by examining native legends and spirituality. But then, I didn't really explore that much, until I came to live in Wales and started writing regularly. That's when I got interested in harps, bards and druids. It also never occurred to me that I might be able to heal old hurts and problems by questing in the inner world. Everything happens at the right time I suppose, although the landscapes around the River Thames in London certainly provided me with some initial landmarks for my journey."

"And since then, you've learned that whenever you care to listen, the land will speak to you wherever you go, have you not? It is simply that most people either choose not to listen, or they have not learned how to do so. By the way," he adds, "your sense of hearing has expanded both inside and outside through your work with counselling and psychotherapy, because you learned to listen. It has also become closely connected to your sense of touch or feeling. Who knows, perhaps one day, you may even stumble across Merlin's house of glass with its many windows and the thirteen treasures of Britain if you stick around long enough."

The angel laughs with a tinkling sound like several bells all ringing together.

"So, tomorrow is the new moon, and except for the stars, the sky will be dark until after Halloween. That means there will be no moonlight to see you in and you won't be able to catch any in your lantern, will you?" I remind him.

"No," the angel replies, "so why not spend some time looking at the stars, or even take a rest from the quest, get some relaxation and enjoy yourself. A lack of moonlight does not mean that I am not there, you can always visualize the moon if you really need my help. Go with the flow, as they say, make life easy for a while," he tells me with a wide smile. The words make me feel more relaxed, more fluid.

"I never thought of that," I tell him, but then I'll probably need space to process tonight's meditation. I have a gut feeling that I'm in for a learning curve on some issue and that there might be alchemy afoot to transmute a leaden obstacle into a golden treasure or an old piece of coal into a new diamond. I've bought a moon calendar for next year, so I can find out exactly how the moon affects my body, my mind and my capacity to be creative during her different phases. For this month, I have looked up the phases on the net and listed their dates.

"So how do you feel now at the end of a waning crescent, standing on the threshold of a new moon?" he asks me.

"I'm physically well and calm, but here in the dark, I am seeding a few new ideas that I hope might grow. I've come to an understanding of late, that the only way with a difficult process is to walk through it since avoidance usually means that it turns up later in a different guise. I'm feeling impatient with anyone who wants too much of my time right now. In fact, I'm feeling downright reclusive."

The angel's tone sounds gentle, compassionate. "Seeds do tend to germinate in the dark, don't they? And you can ask for the space you need without making a fuss. Just tell other people what you need when you need it and get on with anything you have to do."

"Okay, so I need to pause and think, before I open my mouth when I'm in this kind of mood," I answer, "but to change the subject, I have become very aware of a raven, and I have written a poem today. It's about a raven flying into the mysteries."

He doesn't seem in the least bit surprised. "And isn't that a good description of what you are doing in the waning crescent and the dark before the moon begins to wax," he says. "The raven then becomes an internal guide, a good companion during this moon phase. Your body feels fine because you are not refusing to follow. You are letting go and walking into the dark of the new moon. Something buried from the past can be brought out and healed, or you can come to terms with a part of yourself you have neglected. Then, as the moon begins her waxing crescent, you can move on into a new chapter with your treasure. The raven's glittering eye will enable you to see clearly in the dark and she will give you safe passage. Do not forget to keep notes through the moon phases of this month," he reminds me.

"I'll be happy to do that since it was always my intention. Who knows, what inspiration watching the moon might bring me. After all it is how I first became aware of you."

"Then I'll wish you well with your project and leave you to rest for now. If you listen carefully, you might even hear my true name whispered in the wind, sung by a bird or washed ashore on a wave. When you know that, you will not always need to meditate with the moon for I will answer whenever you call."

"Why don't you just tell me yourself?"

"To gather wisdom requires patience and time," he laughs.

"Yes, yes, I know, time does not exist for you, and being patient can slow time down for me."

"In which case it is time to return now."

The angel takes my hand, leading me back through the door in the storm and the wild wind blowing through my everyday autumn reality, before he fades into the dark night along with the moonlight in his lantern. I open my eyes and become aware of the carved wooden raven sitting on my side table under a lamp, which has big round base like a glittering silver ball. I bought that lamp when we first moved into our Welsh home, because it reminded me of a full moon. Soon after, the raven, created by a local woodcarver, touched my soul as soon as I saw it at a craft fair just a few miles away in Barry Town Hall.

I write a few notes, before opening the balcony door, just enough to hear the roaring voices of the wind and the sea, one more time, before I go to bed.

Practice

Many people who experience a connection to the Animal Kingdom through their pets, already have a strong relationship with it. Caring for a pet, helps both children and adults to develop a rapport, as well as a sense of responsibility towards the many other species that share our planet.

If the animal kingdom inspires you, set aside some quiet time to consider the natural world in terms of its creatures, then note the ones that really stand out for you. Now close your eyes and relax to consider them one at a time. What kinds of attributes or qualities does each one of these creatures suggest to you? How exactly do they inspire you?

When the raven appeared to me, I found that I could also employ it as a strong ally in the inner world. Sometimes, then a guide or protector might appear in the inner world as an animal form you are familiar with.

To begin with, select the creature you feel most connected with and try a short meditation on it, keeping your mind open to every impression that flows into the inner world of your imagination. Some people see pictures in their mind's eye, whilst others get impressions of sound, touch, emotion or a scent memory. If you haven't already discovered it on one of your walks, then try to determine which of your senses is the strongest.

You might like to try this exercise whenever you feel a firm link to the Animal Kingdom through any creature you encounter on a wisdom walk or in your garden, especially if it keeps coming back to you like my raven. Standing on a side table in my living room, her carved wooden image evokes ideas of protection, alchemy and inspiration for me when I am working with unresolved issues in my inner and outer worlds. I have found that achieving solutions on the inside eventually reflect on the outside, though not always immediately or in ways I might have expected.

You may also like to try working with a pack of Animal divination cards, as well as your own meditation. The two packs I am familiar with are listed on the resources and further reading pages of this book.

Chapter Eleven

The Gift

Listen

Slow down a while and listen to angel words of making
in the wild wind harmony of waves on rocks and shores
or summer soft breezes blowing high through a pine tree
and frosty night cracklings of warm winter hearth fires,
in the dawn chorus or blackbird's rosy song at twilight
when the sky is ablaze with rubies and coral set into gold
in all seasons, as night flows into day and day into night
new beginnings, endings, a sound of old doors closing,
the first cry of a new-born, the joy of children laughing
the awesome silence of snow-peaks or echoes lost in caves
beneath a moon dream, a star shimmer, a sun gold creation
these songs of making rise in hearts whenever minds lie still,
when you stop your scurrying, worrying, fighting and
wanting
you may hear the angel song in all your deep space places.
Won't you slow down a while and listen?
Iona Jenkins

When I was a child, I knew how to take time out. Children don't
always move in straight lines, they meander about, following
their imaginations. On my way to school, sometimes with other
kids and sometimes alone, I would often veer away from the
main road to wander through a small patch of woodland that
lined the pavement for about two hundred yards, ending at
a busy crossroads, where the lollipop lady (crossing guard)
waited to ensure safe passage. Coming home, I would either
follow the same path again in the opposite direction or I would
walk down a lane, climb over a stile and cut across the fields.

On the way there were tiny fish to watch in a meadow stream, as well as the many different plants and trees, all robed in colors of the season. I loved the land and it loved me back. How exquisite and heady the wild rose with her perfume fit for a queen, decorating the hedgerow. How full of bliss and life the summer in my heart, purple tinged with tufted vetch, red with clover and the pinkish white of tough stemmed yarrow. I lay in the grass, green scented, listening to the bee buzzing honey makers, as I languished content in the smile of a golden sun.

A child's life in Britain during the 1950s and 60s was very different without today's technology. Only six or seven families on our housing estate owned cars, so most people walked. In bad weather, there was a bus stop nearby and two buses an hour passing through our village on their way to Leeds city center. Before the dawn of the mobile phone, or even landlines in every home, we had to communicate from a red phone booth out in the street, where we could also organize a suitable time to take an incoming call. Messages were usually delivered in person and on foot, children ran errands and there was a real sense of security in village life back then, with relatives living close by in a community where people watched out for each other.

I developed a wild independence, because in those days it was also safe for children to be out in the countryside without the constant supervision of adults. People talked to each other, took an interest, so someone always knew where we were. In addition, I always felt shielded in the woods and fields, with a sense that nature herself was taking good care of me.

Growing into adolescence, I left the magic far behind, as I learned to negotiate my way through the outer world of form. I pursued my higher education in the days when access to it was more difficult, but students enjoyed the privilege of a government grant for studying, so that young people from poorer backgrounds did not have to take on the burden of repaying a hefty loan at the end of it. Afterwards, I joined the workforce and embraced city living. Social activities with my peers became far more important to me than nature. Over the years, I worked hard, forgetting how to simply be, becoming an adult doer, until one day, I realized I was exhausted. I sat down and let go, the angels, the land and the spirits of nature were all calling me home.

"Wake up, wake up!" I could hear the demands of my intuitive mind. "You cannot ignore me, or you will burn out."

As soon as I got into this slowing down, making space to walk, to simply be, around my work and social activities, something changed. Rambling along the banks of the tidal Thames, I rediscovered my wild soul in a tale whispered to me by this magic river flowing from a source in the Gloucestershire Cotswolds, where it is known by its original name of Isis, after the Egyptian Mother Goddess.

My thinking mind began to form an alliance with my intuitive one, an internal blending of masculine and feminine, a sacred marriage between the sun and the moon, a process that allows access through that creative golden door. Behind the door lies a garden of possibility, the domain of that magical child from yesterday, who loved to lie in wildflowers listening to the bees. This is where the angels begin to sing my wordscapes into being, where the wise Goddess spins her threads of inspiration for the Bard/Magician to weave into colorful tapestries of poetry, prose or story. I am, therefore, heeding a call to blend the opposites within me, a call for balance as a process that eventually might open wide the golden door of the heart.

During the time I lived in London, I was sometimes moved to paint as well as to write poetry, working purely with color and naïve form since I have neither artistic training nor technical ability. Even so, to my complete surprise, I discovered a few individuals who felt moved, even energized by my untrained efforts at using watercolor and gouache. Although there is an objective technical and organized critique surrounding art, there is also an emotional subjective reaction. I began to paint for sheer joy, and as the angels sang so freely without imposing any rules, I put a few of my pictures into frames and displayed them in our home, as well as giving one or two away.

Learning to work with the angel attitude hasn't been a straightforward process. I soon discovered an internal critic who loved to tell me how I should give up writing poetry and painting my pathetic naïve pictures, because I had no artistic training, so I would never be good enough. This critic would often let the poetry go, but rarely my attempts at painting. One of my friends remarked on the amount of colorful energy the pictures emitted, but I didn't listen to him because he was my friend and I assumed he was humoring me. Then one day, a stranger who came to my home, spied one of my bright naïve pictures hanging on the dining room wall. It was a small painting of a happy golden lion basking in sunshine.

"Who painted that?" she asked, staring at it.

"Me," I replied with some trepidation, expecting her to laugh.

The response was unexpected. "Can I buy it from you?" she asked. "It has something really cheerful and warm that appeals to me."

I was so taken aback, I felt awkward.

"But it isn't worth anything," I told her nervously. "I was just having fun, and anyway, I wouldn't know what to charge, except for the price of the frame." My self-effacing attitude forced me to miss out on a spontaneous opportunity. She was feeling an emotional pull towards the golden lion, and on some level, it might even have been energetically useful to her. I felt my cheeks burning and I didn't sell it to her, so I have no way of knowing what might have happened next had I responded to that request. What I understand now, is that individuals sometimes have spontaneous emotional responses to art. True inspiration, like that lightning bolt from the blue, is by its very nature instantaneous. It follows then, that overcautious individuals might do well to free up their own spontaneity, to break it out of the prison imposed by a controlling internal critic.

The fact that I have not painted much since I left London is not because I have given it up, but rather because my joy of writing has taken over and I have developed a preference for painting in words. I have, however, used my pictures on the covers of a fantasy trilogy I wrote for adolescents when I first began to turn my inspiration into books. My website designer liked the rainbow tree I painted for the front of the third book, which I called *The Garden of Possibility*, so much, that he asked my permission to make a poster of it for his wall. Perhaps then, that cover might just embody some of the possibilities of the title it illustrates.

Every day, I am learning to be more generous with gifting, in bringing inspiration from the heart world into the outer world of form. I have become more and more willing to create for the sheer joy of it. Doing that doesn't exactly silence the critic, but over the years its voice has changed, it has learned to give constructive feedback instead of beating me up. Who can really say, how much or how little of the positive art we create may benefit others or begin to brighten the color of a single thread in the complex fabric of our world? Who can say how many ripples one seemingly insignificant little stone can cause on the still smooth surface of a lake?

We have a long way to go in our evolution as human beings, but if we can aspire to becoming whole human beings in a blend of body, mind and spirit, instead of denying our amazing human life in the search for some transcendental state of perfection, then we might begin to feel complete, creative and at home in the universe. The world's parameters are constantly changing, some creations may stand the test of time, whereas others may crumble after only a short period. Ultimately, all form passes, as illustrated by statues of the Hindu God Nataraja dancing in a circle of flames through the continuous cycles of birth, life and death, and back to birth again in ever-changing dynamic energy. This image gives the impression that we can all choose to join in the dance.

I create from my life force in the present, though I might use ideas from the past or aspirations for the future. I know that some aspects of my art might only have a brief life, whilst others could last much longer. I have little control over the outcome, so again, I must let go of my creation once it is complete. What I have understood is that my ability to create grows more substantial, the stronger my connection becomes, as I tune in and increase my skills to speak the language of angels in my own way.

The more I take time out, relax, employ my senses, merge with our wonderful planet and its place in the greater universe, then my understanding of the Great Song and my own creative life grows in proportion. I find an angel to teach me wisdom in the moonlight, a raven to guide and protect me through the dark spaces in the unconscious, to change the base metal of shadow obstacles and challenges into gold. I find that the tree spirits nurture me, so that there is wisdom and guidance in every wood. Outside my window, ideas, images, and answers break upon the shore with the waves of an incoming tide and I can banish old anxieties by using my imagination to cast them into the sea, to be washed away when the tide goes out again. The angels will speak to my heart through the whole of nature, whenever I am open enough to allow them in, whenever I dive without fear into the stream of Awen.

Nature also offers her gifts without hesitation. Within a single acorn gifted by an oak, there is already the promise of a great tree with roots to stabilize the soil, a sturdy trunk with spreading branches for birds to nest in, leaves that help to regulate oxygen in the ecosystem and new acorns to keep the life cycle going. The entire future possibility of that tree lies hidden in every seed.

And just like that acorn, today's people are the fruits of a long line of ancestors. We are the gift in the present, we can learn from the past and create a great future from what we do in the now since we are an evolving species. To quote from the Buddha again, "With our thoughts we create the world." Mind needs to work through heart so that our creative thoughts arise from a sea of love, speaking and singing in the language of angels.

Gifting

Be who you are, not what others think you ought to be.
Teach your internal critic the art of constructive dialogue
Unlock the prison in your mind to free your spontaneity
Seek the magical child in your internal garden of possibility
where angels are continually singing your life into being
since you are both their art, and glorious gift to the world
the heart listens and creates with love from life's passion.

Practice

Look into your heart. Is there something you really want to create from your love and your life's passion? What beautiful gift do you yearn to bring from your inner landscape into the world of form? Remember that the size of the gift is of no importance right now, and that if only one person ever appreciates and benefits from it, then you will be making a difference however small. In time, creativity will grow and flourish like a strong tree or a radiant flower from this first tiny seedling.

If you have the beginnings of an idea that has not yet grown enough to push above ground into a creative project, then take some time each day to water the fruit of your first effort with a little meditation, work, or both, until that shoot finally appears. When it does, don't waste its life force by talking about it too much, or giving away your idea. Be patient and keep feeding your seedling until it blooms for you.

Equally, try not to get involved in critical internal dialogue that causes frost to wither your plant at this crucial stage. When the fruit is fully ripe, then you can seek constructive feedback from trustworthy souls. Try to work for the sake of love and enjoyment, making changes on your own by learning to appraise your efforts constructively. There is no hurry, impatience will make you cut corners and erode the quality of your work. Allow your gift to unfold steadily by taking time out as often as you need to. Remember to celebrate every moment of your love's growth from its heart seed.

Chapter Twelve

Dancing the Circle

Around and Around
The wheel is turning
the season changing
as the door opens
and my path goes on
to new stars birthing
I am dancing the circle
around and around.
Iona Jenkins

Although I had easy access to nature, I cannot in all honesty say that my childhood was idyllic, but I do consider myself very lucky to have grown up in a village. Although we lived in a mining area, there was at that time, a strong village community life based around the Victorian stone built primary school, that my father had attended before me, as well as a church and activities at the village hall, which all helped to create a sense of order within the community. As I mentioned earlier, my father in resisting the pleas of the priest, had chosen not to enroll me in the newly built Catholic school on the outskirts of a town six miles away.

"The local school was good enough for me," he had said, "and therefore, it's good enough for her. We don't need to be bothered with any extra religion."

I was, in fact, happy where I was, though I suspect that my parents' decision had little to do with any informed choice about the quality of education that either of the schools could provide. It was more than likely based on my father's total dislike of our Catholic parish priest at that time. However, opting for the village school meant that my nature kingdom with its abundance of green space and woodland would always be there for me at the end of my school day and I would not have to waste time riding on a bus.

In any event, my local school education turned out very well. I had competent teachers, who were keen to acknowledge our village environment and the changing seasons with the presence of a nature table in every classroom. Members of my form brought gifts for our classroom table, both from our own foraging and from nature walks with the teacher. We were encouraged to press wildflowers, to find out about animals, birds and insects by creating projects, which involved exploring, writing and drawing. We sang seasonal songs and hymns, we also enjoyed seasonal painting and crafts. We planted bulbs indoors and seeds in a small strip of land that had been marked out into tiny circular plots. My awareness and love of nature grew like a strong tree, alongside my knowledge and intellect.

The school was situated in the center of the village, about a mile from my home. As stated in the previous chapter there were two routes from which to choose. I could either walk a mile along tarmac and paved footpaths following the main road, or meander across the fields from the back of our housing estate. After the last stile, of the field walk, the final leg of the journey included a picturesque lane boasting several old stone cottages with stunning gardens, a stream and the Doctor's surgery. Most days, I opted for the main road route on my way to school, but I often preferred to return through the fields when the weather and the earth were dry.

There were also my beloved trees to visit if I chose to follow the main road. Situated to one side of the pavement, the small plot of woodland was alive with birdsong, fresh green shoots and buds in spring. In summer heat, the trees provided a cool green sanctuary and in the autumn a treasure trove of beechnuts and acorns to collect for necklace making, or red-brown horse chestnuts for a game of conkers. The world outside was beautiful and exciting, bringing me warmth, comfort, joy and magic. Even in winter when snow covered the branches, when I had to wear mittens fixed to my coat sleeves with elastic and wool-lined zip-up black suede boots to keep my feet dry, the red berries and the robin's breast glowed warm and red like fire against the ice.

Although these impressions were filed in my memory at an early age and although I am not much inclined to make acorn necklaces or play conkers today, I do, of course, remain open to the experiences and inspiration that each season brings to enrich my adult years. If I had to live in a land where the seasonal change was not such an obvious fact of life, then I would likely miss the experience. I try not to complain about the weather. When it is cold, I put on a coat and go out regardless, for I know that any inspiration will light me up with its flames of enthusiasm. I always discover something that I had not been aware of before, even when following a familiar path. The world is in a continuous state of renewal, inviting me to join in and celebrate her colors, light, sound, textures, elements. How could I possibly resist?

At the time of writing this chapter autumn steadily draws to its close. The weather has turned cold with the Winter Solstice just three weeks away. This year, the season has been wet and stormy. Those bright days, when the sun shines through the golds, ambers, russets and crimsons of dying leaves, have been few and far between, but this week I am lucky. The light may be fading, as the earth's orbit moves the northern hemisphere away from the sun, but today's sunset paints the water and sky in spectacular deep rose, dove and charcoal grey, bestowing a soft compassionate quality on the quiet ocean outside my window, now that the storms have all blown away.

Autumn is the time for letting go, a time to surrender after a fruitful harvest, a time when the soul seeks to shed all that is worn out, just as a tree sheds its leaves to survive, blossom and thrive again in the Spring. I reflect upon my harvest, on the fruits of my labor that I have gathered and stored in my barn. This year I have learned more than one life lesson and gained new wisdom. I have consolidated friendships and I have met new people. I have found my poet's voice and made progress in turning what was once both a poem and the beginning of an idea, into this book. I have also succeeded in having another four of my poems published.

In the old Celtic calendar, the 31st of October marked the end of the year with the festival of Samhain, which is also known today as All Souls, All Hallows or Halloween. The first day of the Celtic new year on the first of November marked the beginning of winter, before the solstice on the twenty-first of December. The seasons on the wheel of the year can be illustrated by a circle with an equal-armed cross inside to divide it up into four quarters. Autumn is traditionally placed on the left of the circle, its direction being west, its quality being wisdom, its Archangel of the directions Gabriel and its element water.

I see the water element as cleansing, washing away all that is worn out or finished, so that my angels may bring the ingredients for a new brew of Awen to stir in the goddess Ceridwen's cauldron. If it splashes on my fingers as inspiration, then the Goddess may chase me like the boy Gwion in the Welsh legend of Taliesin, who was forced to transform himself through each of the four elements before he could be reborn as a great Bard (see chapter 14 for full story). I do understand that I must sometimes make changes if I want to create something of value.

Poets rarely starve in dusty attic rooms for their art today, but this legend might just explain why more sensitive creative types often run a gauntlet of emotional difficulties before they succeed in producing something worthwhile. There are periods of transition when we are required to let go of worn-out beliefs to find wisdom or gain deeper understanding. Autumn is a great time for achieving this. Sometimes beautiful things can be born in desperate places.

Then comes the winter, a time of patience, of waiting, a time of opening to new growth, as the seeds I have planted deep under the frozen earth begin struggling to reach the surface. After letting go of all that is complete and shedding that which is worn out, I am resting, renewing myself, taking advantage of this pause when the Earth is still, so that I can store enough energy to grow again when the light returns. I sometimes increase my walking pace to keep warm outside, but in general I find myself slowing down, meditating more, enjoying relaxation and warmth in my home with the grey sea outside, rippling or roaring, beyond the stark black outlines of bare trees on the edge of the cliff, where winter seagulls hide behind the mist and wail like phantoms on the wind.

But all through this time, my heart is ablaze, and vibrant as that robin's breast. The creative potion is almost ready to spill out into spring. I have learned to love the snow when it falls, to relish its deep silence, when the stars shine bright and warm in a black ice sky above white landscapes, so quiet, that I sometimes find myself lulled into dreams. I feed visiting birds on my balcony, so they too may live to sing again in Spring.

My inner winter is not a sorrowful time, as I am aware of the heart fire, heating the angel brew singing in the magic cauldron. I locate the winter season in the north, with the element of earth on my wheel of the year. Bright white stars in frosty heavens sometimes almost seem to be attached to me by threads of silver light. Winter is a season that evokes images of breathtaking beauty through my inner vision. I have learned to seek that hidden light, which is the lamp of the Archangel Uriel, shining in the dark, illuminating the door that leads onwards to sun return and the promise of new life. I welcome it as a friend.

"Time to wake up!" the winds of early March are shouting through the branches, scurrying the clouds, stirring the senses. In my inner world the potion is ready to be decanted, whilst outside, primroses, crocuses and daffodils are bursting to tell their story in shades of butter, amethyst, gold, white and lemon. Angels and birds are all spring singing in this time of the making, of creatures birthing and my pen flowing with poetry.

The landscape transforms as the earth puts on her coat of fresh spring green, all dotted with daisy faces. Spring is a time of renewal, a time of hope for all. In this fertile growing garden, anything is possible. My energy soars high with the sun, as I change into lighter clothes to match my mood. In this season the angel voice is louder, the stream of inspiration flows faster, keeping my pen busy with word pictures. Spring, located in the East like the rising sun on the wheel of the year, is linked to the Archangel Raphael who brings healing and renewal with the element of air, which is why my being always feels lighter.

I love blossoms. Almond, cherry, and apple, like a thick sugary coating completely covering every single branch in fondant pink, ivory or dazzling white. Unable to resist the sweet smell of lilac, I cannot pass by one of these trees without stopping to savor the scent of its dripping blossoms. The perfume evokes memories of earlier lilac trees in gardens of the past belonging to my grandparents. Later in the season, I find pleasure walking in woods carpeted with bluebells. Here is the scent of a blue-lit heaven, elevating my senses and raising my awareness to the possibility of otherworldly realms that intermingle with my earth life and write themselves into existence.

The warmth of the summer sun is like a soothing balm for my muscles and bones. Life becomes easier, movement more fluid. I can sit outside and drift into meditation or a contented daydream. Passionate summer is located on the south of the wheel with the element of fire and the Archangel Michael.

This season means sparkling morning seas and warm nights of glittering stars in indigo skies. I can get out my walking sandals and let my toes breathe. I can put away my boots and hang up my winter waterproof coat. The sun infuses my skin, turning it light gold with solar life force. This is a time of leisure and freedom, a time to rest from hard work, a time to play, as the corn and fruits ripen. The green of the land has matured and deepened with intense vitality.

This bright warm weather encourages positive mind states. I am optimistic, focused on success, passionate about life. I relax easily into my imagination, because my body is willing to move at a slower pace, to find resonance with the higher temperature, allowing more space for images to arise from the inner life. In summer, I have more outdoor time to listen to the angels speaking through the web of creation. In this season, I often pen handwritten first drafts outside, either on my balcony, facing the sea with its tides flowing between worlds or in a local park, under the shade of a friendly tree, where my imagination can catch its inspiration from a passing breeze. This is when those seeded ideas, nurtured in the earth's winter cauldron and pushed above ground in the Spring, now begin to bear fruit, which will ripen for the harvest.

I might begin a new writing project at any time, but I can always illustrate the way I like to map it out, by employing my image of the wheel of the year, which I have also heard referred to as a sun cross. The later Christian Celtic cross is a more elaborate version of this. I have found four words to describe each of its quadrants in terms of my own creative process. These are Innovation, Creation, Consolidation and Celebration.

INNOVATION comes in winter's dark, when seeded ideas are nurtured, in the warmth of the cauldron, shaping themselves ready to push above the earth. It is important not to force growth as ideas might be lost and die before they are mature enough to rise to the surface. Any preparatory research is carried out in this phase. I make notes to add to any lines I might have written previously and stored.

CREATION follows in the Spring as ideas expand and begin to shape themselves into a manuscript with a title.

CONSOLIDATION happens in Summer, when all the elements from my previous efforts are blended, as the project comes to fruition and the editing starts.

CELEBRATION is for Autumn when work is finished, my creative harvest gathered in, and I begin to clear all traces of it from my inner garden to make the ground ready to receive the seeds of a new venture.

A friend once said to me that putting the finishing touches to a completed book is like giving birth. I create something, grow it, nurture it, before sending it out into the world to fend for itself. I think it important to design a short ritual ceremony for celebrating the release of all completed artistic endeavors to create a positive atmosphere for sending the newborn written child on its way.

To everything there is a season and a time to every purpose under heaven.
Ecclesiastes, Chapter 3, Verse 1, KJV Bible

Practice

Draw a circle with an equal-armed cross inside it, then write the names of each season in its appropriate quadrant. I prefer to begin with winter in the North and work clockwise to East, South, West, and back to North.

Now consider each season in turn and either using the space on your diagram or if you need more, then use a separate page. Write down every association that comes to you for each quarter of your year. If you wish, you could also dedicate a corner of your living space to celebrating the season. Think about color, plant, candle, leaf and/or seed, wood, fabric, pottery, crystal, words, picture or whatever feels right for you.

Next focus on the current season and plan a wisdom walk, either locally or further afield if you prefer, remembering to record your sensory impressions and ideas. If you have access to an outdoor labyrinth then you might prefer to do seasonal labyrinth walks. You can also give finger labyrinth walks a seasonal theme.

Later, if it feels right, you might like to attempt a meditation to locate this current season in the inner world of your imagination, so that you can compare your inner and outer experiences.

What is the season telling you, and is there some practical way you would like to work with it either emotionally, creatively, or both?

Chapter Thirteen

Moon Goddess

Snow Moon
Full moon white robed
soft edges submerged
in swirling cloud banks
thick and light as snow
flying over the high tide
like mild winter ghosts
on the night air surging
and the salt spray rising
exhilarating, free and wild
two stars wink and sparkle
from black velvet spaces
at the end of the storm
Iona Jenkins

Tonight, I sense a completely different atmosphere. I have
never seen the sea and the full moon together in quite the same
way before. A storm named Ciara arrived, bringing some very
difficult weather conditions sweeping across the British Isles. I
must add though, that the wind speeds in my area turned out
to be considerably lower than those predicted on last night's
weather forecast. We have been lucky on this stretch of the
South Wales coast. Heavy rain, however, has forced me to stay
indoors all day, but fortunately, I am also enjoying an increase
in my flow of inspiration, brought on by the presence and light
of tonight's full moon.

It is almost midnight and full moons keep me awake. Tonight,
she is surrounded by banks of shape-shifting silver grey and
white clouds, creating an effect that reminds me of snow. An

occasional star sparkles from tiny black velvet spaces left by the moving clouds and the pearl white beams of this February light. I am prompted to do an Internet search and soon discover that Native American tribes referred to this second full moon of winter, as Snow Moon.

Even with the intermittent lashing rain and turbulent sea, the temperature is relatively mild. As soon as there is a temporary lull in the rain, I venture out on to my balcony. The wind blows wild through my hair, refreshing my face, as I melt into the sound of invisible waves crashing against the dark shoreline and the taste of salted air on every breath. Finally, I close the door and light my candle lantern, a beacon to guide me in the storm. I experience a feeling of gentle whiteness, like light on snow that continues to enfold me even when I go inside and secure the door. This has got to be an angel night. I close my eyes and drift into the waking dream.

"Are you there, Angel?" I ask, already knowing what the answer will be.

"You can always find me in the moonlight and a Snow Moon is no exception," comes the answer.

"Your presence feels more feminine tonight," I observe. "I am getting an impression of a woman dressed in a flowing white garment, which has what looks like either a hood or a shawl of some kind covering her hair."

"As you are already aware, I am not bound by the limitations of time, space, form or even gender. You set the scene and I respond, meeting you where you are. Right now, Snow Moon on water at this threshold place, is evoking sacred feminine energy for you, in the form of a pearl white light lady, a moon goddess, who offers you entry into her sanctuary of peace and healing, at the center of the storm. Here you may experience stillness of mind with space for wisdom to blossom. Always be sure to let her know that she is most welcome for that is a good form of spiritual politeness in greeting any positive influence.

Are you ready to continue with this?" the angel asks kindly.

"Yes," I reply, "but first let me think thoughts of welcome to the lady and the moon. By the way, Angel," I add, "you too are most welcome."

The angel smiles and bows his head in recognition. "I thank you," he says in a cheerful and respectful tone of voice.

"And right now," I continue, "I am experiencing a great wave of peace, as soft as swan's down or dove feathers. Such a contrast to all that heaving crashing water caused by today's stormy weather."

"And this peace remains constant," says the angel, "regardless of whatever might be happening on your planet, whether it is whipping winds, covering cloud, surging seas or anything else. This pearl white lady of the moon you see, will give you refuge in the eye of the storm, which as you know is always a place of calm. Well, that is, of course, if you remember to seek her sanctuary, before you have a chance to stray from your path and lose yourself in a maze of worry and anxious thoughts. Now tell me, how exactly do you intend to make that connection when we are not working?"

"I suppose that I could remember tonight's image of the Snow Moon with the pearly clouds and think of the word peace at the same time," I answer without thinking too much.

"Just so. Your world can be a turbulent place and I am not just referring to the weather. There are oceans of chaotic thoughts and feelings whirling around in the atmosphere since so many of you humans seem to have untold difficulty moderating your negative emotions and reactions. Peace and wisdom work well together," the angel reminds me, "so try to float your consciousness on the word *peace*. What kind of impressions come to you, in addition to the white lady of the Snow Moon?"

"I see full moonlight, of course, on a field of snow, soft pearly clouds, flocks of gentle cooing doves, a lake, smooth and still as glass with a white swan sailing. There are white stargazer lilies and roses that I can almost smell, a patch of snowdrops, lily of the valley, a silver chalice, a string of pearls, a white five-pointed star, white candles and a tinkling of silver bells. The colors in this scene, then, are all white, silver and pearl. At the same time, I am reminded of a short poem I wrote in the gardens of Syon Park, when I lived in London. I have a vivid recollection of sitting by the lake on a hot summer's day, observing an artist busily sketching on the opposite bank, when I had a clear impression of a full moon reflected in the water, even though it was daylight, and later, I picked up a delicate scent of white lilies, as I began to walk away. That poem, called 'Syon Park', is in *Heartsong*, my first book of poetry and reflections. I think the white lady and I are not strangers. And there is also something I once read about this place," I add, latching on to a sudden memory as it fluttered through my mind like a singing bird.

"According to a guidebook I bought several years ago, Syon Park, a London Estate owned by the Duke of Northumberland in Brentford, Middlesex, takes its name from Syon Abbey. This former powerful religious institution dedicated to St. Brigit and the Virgin Mary, had once occupied that site, until 1539 when it became a casualty of King Henry VIII's monastery dissolution campaign, after his split with the Church in Rome. Named after Mount Zion in the Holy Land, this influential Brigettine establishment owned substantial acres of land, as well as a vast collection of religious books and manuscripts, which made it an important center for spiritual learning.

Following this thread of thought further, I have recently heard local church bells pealing for Candlemas, the festival of St. Brigit or St. Bride, which in the Christian calendar celebrates the return of the sun. In the Celtic calendar, this time also marks the festival of Imbolc, Brighid, goddess of poetry and healing. I begin to sense a link between my white moon lady, the scent of lilies blending with the images and the creativity happening around Syon Lake on that sunny day."

"See how the connections come to you when we talk? What exactly do you think is happening, when you actively let those pictures, sounds and scents flow through your inner senses into the word *peace*?" he asks.

"*Peace* ceases to be just a word when I do that, it somehow becomes energized. The impressions give it life and my whole being responds. My mind is cooled, as still as that lake in Syon, the atmosphere is gentle and silent except for an occasional feint impression of tinkling silver bells. There is no internal chatter, as I sit in my white flower-scented, candlelit heart space, merging with the Snow Moon in its soft clouds above my head. I could stay here forever."

"So, you have been able to take a simple word, to give it life and meaning by allowing symbolic material to flow through your imagination. The atmosphere is very real, you have invoked your own sanctuary and there is your magic."

"Simple and yet powerful enough to create peace," I observe, remembering to mentally welcome the presence of the Goddess again since I have just invoked her. "That also makes me question whether a poem, or a piece of prose using these images might ease anxiety, maybe even lower blood pressure, and if speaking those peace words as a guided meditation might also add to their effectiveness. I wonder whether I am beginning to get an idea of the poetic and the healing possibilities the energy of Brighid, or St. Bride might offer us."

"You have responded to the conditions outside, using the flow of inspiration they bring in your own way and as a result, you have linked into a greater flow of creative ideas to complement your poetry," says the angel. "We are meeting in your heart space, through moonlight on water, as we so often do, but tonight, you had already synchronized with that Snow Moon before you looked up any information about it. Therefore, in my opinion, your connection might be a little stronger than you actually think it is."

"And do you also speak to me through the trees?" I ask, remembering how much inspiration comes to me on woodland walks.

"The whole of the natural world, and that includes the universe, transmits its wisdom in the language of angels, the Creative Spirit flows through all that exists, but you are also required to tune in with your heart if you are seeking to understand the love, which accompanies such wisdom. Nature does not experience the separation that you have mistakenly created for yourselves. As you once discovered with the art in Rome, we also speak through every positive human creation, because we belong to its source. It pays to listen and to feel more, instead of just talking all the time. Try to connect your thoughts and feelings, practice the art of simply being, whenever you have enough space to relax your body and mind."

I spend a few minutes, mulling over the angel's words before I continue.

"There is a lot of material on the market related to positive thinking, but what you have helped me to understand, is that positive words work better for me, when I can add images, scents and sounds, feelings that evoke the essence of that word. What I mean is that the whole word picture I have painted, is more effective for me than a simple spoken or written word. It's the sensory material that gives the word a meaning that extends beyond the intellect, isn't it? That is how I was able to experience peace in my whole being."

"Of course," the angel agrees, "and as you use your words in a descriptive way to paint pictures, let us try another one," he sounds enthusiastic. "Might I suggest *celebration*? Relax and let the word drift through your senses."

I do what he asks and soon find myself drifting into an internal summer season.

"I have an image of bright bees buzzing on abundant lavender flowers trailing over a stone wall. This image, which comes from a garden I passed during a summer walk, inspired a poem. The sweet taste of honey, mead, the scent of beeswax candles, a joyful Irish band with a bodhran drum, vibrant carnival colors, dancing, sunshine and laughter. All of these impressions relate to celebration for me since they evoke a feeling of joy."

"Humans need to celebrate everything that is good, because it enhances both their energy and happiness. This kind of word picture could certainly help to lift a depressed mood and increase feelings of optimism. This idea of celebration could also be expressed through any kind of art such as weaving, pottery, painting, music, dance, wood carving, fabrics and fashion, cookery and so on, according to personal preference and talent. Can you add two more examples of word pictures from your poetry?"

"I really had a sense of the word *plenty* when I wrote harvest poems using images of golden ripe wheat fields shining in the sun, to create an impression of a generous Earth Mother, providing nourishment. Right now, I can also conjure up the scent of apples cut in half to reveal the seeded star at the center and the taste of soft blackberries, eaten straight from the hedgerow, that leave purple juice stains on fingers. My wordscapes expand with the impressions I have stored in my subconscious files, as well as with the new ones I am open to receive."

"As I am now in full flight with this exercise," I tell the angel, smiling, "it is appropriate that my next symbol is a bird then. A seagull is the first image that comes to mind with the word *freedom*. The bird evokes a sense of freedom on all levels for me, physical, emotional, mental, and spiritual, especially when it flies in summer blue skies. I have loved the cry of seagulls since I was a child in England, because it used to signify a day trip to the seaside, a week's holiday in August on the east coast of Yorkshire in a caravan or chalet, the feeling of wet sand between my toes, as I collected shells or paddled in the cool North Sea, immersed in the sound of gentle waves foaming and flowing over the shoreline. Today, I watch the gulls from my balcony in Wales, as they float on the wind, or fly high over the ocean, in joyful unfettered freedom. They help me to step back from my chattering mind and relax." I sigh with contentment in this sense of free space and detachment I have invoked for myself.

"These images speak to you, but of course," the angel reminds me, "anyone can find his or her own level in a treasury of symbolic language. Seagull is poetic for you, but someone with a different talent or temperament might only view this bird as a noisy nuisance. For a poet, images evoke words and in turn words evoke more images. Words energized by sensory impressions from your creative imagination enable you to paint in words, so it's little wonder that some of the color words you use, can also be found on artists' paint tubes."

"And I do love the names of paint colors," I tell him. "You have helped me to understand that positive words are powerful when energized with feeling and sensory impressions. However, I can also see how energizing negative words might be destructive to ourselves, to others, to our world. It's what you said about the oceans of negative thoughts and emotions. Sometimes the stress in our minds can lead us into that without saying anything out loud, causing us to pollute our own atmosphere and the atmospheres of those around us. Could this be why some places or people feel heavy and off-putting, whilst others seem to be light and welcoming?"

"This is definitely going in the right direction," the angel tells me. "So please continue, for I am sure that you have more to say on this subject."

"Yes, and I understand now, why Tibetan Buddhism emphasizes *right speech*. I came up with an idea of painting with words. An idea of creating wordscapes to inspire, to open the doors of awareness that is motivated by a sincere desire to lift the spirit, heal the soul, increase intuition, and transmit the peace, which today has risen with the moon, in my flow of inspiration. To work with this creative spirituality, I understand that I might be required to continue developing a wise intellect to mold all that heart energy into the words I aspire to put into my writing. It isn't always going to be a smooth ride, is it? But this is how I have chosen to live my life as an artist."

"That is what I had hoped you would say," the angel replies, "for that is also my own intention, though I would never interfere with your free will. Until our next conversation, then, I'll let you get on with energizing your positive words. This aligns with the word alchemy you first came up with in the woodland, moving it to yet another new level by adding sensory impressions, that allow you to feel and see the words as they flow through you when you write. Are you still experiencing the peace you encountered at the start of our conversation?" he asks.

"Totally, and the impression of the white lady remains with me, though my intention is to draw an imaginary curtain and detach from this Snow Moon experience, as soon as our evening together comes to a close."

He nods with satisfaction, "Then may her influence increase and continue to infuse your life with peace and all the inspiration you need."

And with that he is already fading back into the moonlight. Even after I open my eyes and take up my pen to write, that peace remains constant, though the angel's creative wisdom is complete for tonight. I acknowledge that I am tired, but nevertheless, I want to finish my notes before I retire. Task over, I glance at the clock. It is 2:15 in the morning and this Snow Moon will reach its fullest at 2:23. My emotions are a still lake, my mind feels as cool and silent as moonlight on snow, sweet as white lilies, soft as a cloud bank. With some reluctance, I turn away from the moon's pearly brightness, draw my imaginary curtain and head off to bed for a deep, peaceful night's sleep.

Practice

Think about using a moon calendar to map out the moon phases for the next month. You can find one on a site called *moonphases. co.uk*. Now check out your physical and emotional energy with each of the moon's phases during a 28-day period. Remember that since the moon moves the tides, this celestial mystic Goddess is sure to move the water contained within the human body, which can vary from around 40 to 70 percent according to age and gender. This is the reason she influences our energy levels and tugs at the emotions, either lighting up the shadows of issues we have yet to resolve or bathing our wisdom and love in a soft angel light. (See the angel conversation in chapter 17.)

Therefore, the responsibility is yours, to meditate with the moon if it feels right for you. If you are not drawn to the moon at this time, then stick to noticing how it affects your physical energy and moods as suggested at the beginning of this exercise. It is especially important to keep it simple if you are physically ill or experiencing any kind of mental or emotional turmoil.

Chapter Fourteen

Land and Legend

Yr Wyddfa

A deep silence cloaks the summit
of Yr Wyddfa rising into cloud
the lower peaks and green valleys
of misted Eryri wind around me
like a vast coiling earth dragon
I have taken a step closer to heaven
where my soul flies with the eagles
and angels soaring on wind songs
wings of gold and a sun shimmer.
Iona Jenkins

I would like to relate a tale of two summers ago, when my husband, who is interested in vintage railways, expressed a wish to ride on the steam train, from Llanberis in the Snowdonia National Park to the summit of Yr Wyddfa/Mount Snowdon. Now railways in themselves, hold no passion for me except as a means of travel, but since I do enjoy places that are rich in legend, as well as some suggestion of magic, I agreed that a few days away around my birthday would allow me to combine a holiday with a modest celebration. Here was a chance for us to plan a brilliant trip that would bring our individual interests together.

The Snowdonia National Park or Eryri, as it is known locally, is a wild beautiful landscape, steeped in myth and oozing enough magical possibility to capture any fertile imagination. A historical land of druids and bards, it holds the promise of a poet's paradise. Eryri and Yr Wyddfa, the names in Welsh are a singing dragon, an echo from the land itself, and when

I pronounce them, it is as though they possess the power to transport me into something beyond just a popular tourist spot. The words form a bridge that links my imagination with the past. I am sensing a magical empowering quality in the musical sound of these descriptive Welsh place names, as the language resonates with the soul of the land. Their English equivalents Mount Snowdon and Snowdonia evoke in me quite a different mood that keeps my imagination in the present, but as English is my own language, I also wonder whether I might be able to find inspiration for new stories and poems in these words too. I decide that names are important and hold power, whatever language they may be spoken in.

Staying with the Welsh language and my link to the past for now, I am reminded again of Taliesin, who is said to have been the greatest bard in Wales, and I begin to understand how such a legend could have originated in this region. Seeking the source of the story, we begin our journey at Llyn Tegid/Lake Bala, a vast long body of water with its own little railway circuit, that today provides holidays for people who enjoy sailing and canoeing. There are swimmers and water sport enthusiasts rather than bards. Nevertheless, I am determined to renew the tradition, if only for myself, by taking that step back in time in search of Taliesin.

We are staying at a friendly hotel situated on Bala High Street. The food is tasty and the room, although quite small, is comfortable with a pleasant atmosphere, a good shower and soft towels. It feels exactly right, so I am already enthusiastic. Most of the locals I meet in shops and cafés, speak Welsh to each other, though being bilingual, they switch easily to English for visitors. I enjoy hearing spoken Welsh on the street, it brings me closer to Eryri, and although a strong Christian tradition in this village has replaced the druids of old, I sense that their presence has not been completely wiped from the landscape. I am seeking echoes of those memories, hidden in remote valleys, on mountain peaks, recorded in the rocks and whispered through the water lapping against the shores of Llyn Tegid.

Questioning a few of Bala's inhabitants, I discover that the legend of Taliesin has been largely forgotten in the village today. Whatever happened to those traditional stories, rising from the soul of this mountainous terrain? Stories, which might have once rung around fires in bardic voices, passing down the generations in the language of this land. At the same time, I have no doubt there are modern bards and storytellers, who continue to be inspired by such an incredible landscape. I am hoping to write poetry in the present, to pick up my own tiny drops of Awen as they spill from the Goddess's cauldron, like Taliesin of the legendary past.

It is my birthday, and I am standing on the shores of Llyn Tegid. This is a busy area of the lake, a place of joyous earth and holidaymaking, situated at the end of the village. There are ice cream vendors, a café, boating equipment, swimmers, people relaxing in deck chairs, dogs, fishermen and barefoot children, all enjoying the water at summer's end while the weather lasts.

As I change my focus from the outer world to fix my senses on the view down the length of the lake towards the mountains, the soft September sunshine strokes my skin with a gold-dipped paintbrush. The temperature remains warm, but I am already aware of a change, a waning of the sun's power, as it travels towards the equinox, coloring tinges of autumn russet into treetop and root. I can taste it tepid on the breeze and hear it in every note of birdsong weaving through this land of seasons that turn and turn again through the wheel of the year.

I remove my shoes to experience the solid support of earth against the soles of my feet, connecting soft and vulnerable to the hard, pebbled shore, reminding me to stay grounded. I step into the water, soft and caressing as silk. The sand grains ooze between my toes, as I wade until the lake is lapping against my calves. I wobble a bit, unstable at first, before my mind surrenders to the magic. Still like a heron waiting for a fish, I breathe three times, pulling my consciousness into the heart. The breeze blows and the water flows through my wild soul with a feeling of lightness, until I scarcely seem to exist. I am softening around the edges, merging with the landscape. The legend of Taliesin becomes a moving image on the screen of my imagination, inspiring me to relate the Bard's tale to you:

Not so far from a cave where King Arthur and his knights lay sleeping, there was once a secret city called Dinas Affaraon located in the highest peaks of Ereyri, where a band of druid alchemists known as the Fferyllt were thought to hold the secret for brewing an elixir they called Awen. This was a magical potion that could enlighten and inspire anyone who tasted it, with only three drops. At that time an important lady, who was really the Goddess Ceridwen, lived by a lake with her husband Lord Tegid. They had two children, a girl of incredible beauty named Creirwy, and a son called Afagddu (sometimes also known as Morfran) whose name means Utter Darkness. The latter was, in fact, such a hideous-looking child that Lord Tegid, who could scarcely bear a single glance in his direction, traveled far and wide, staying away from home as often as he possibly could.

To help her son, Ceridwen decided that she would seek to make him both wise and inspired, as compensation for his hideous looks. And so, she made the journey to Dinas Affaraon to beg the druid alchemists to give her the formula for their precious elixir of Awen.

The Fferyllt did in fact grant her request, willingly passing on their knowledge, complete with precise instructions to fill a cauldron with fresh water and to collect various herbs to be picked at certain times of the day and night, according to the positions of the sun and the moon. She was told then, to boil the mixture on the shores of the lake for a year and a day, until at the end of that time, three drops of the elixir would fly from the cauldron to be bottled for Afagddu's benefit.

On returning home, Ceridwen prepared the mixture in her cauldron, before employing two men, who then came to live in a hut by the lake. The young man whose name was Gwion and the old man known as Morda were given the task of watching over and stirring the cauldron, but they were also strictly forbidden to ever taste of its contents.

For a full year they tended the fire and stirred that cauldron, until the goddess arrived with her son on its final day of brewing. As misfortune would have it, the old man Morda, as well as Ceridwen and Afagddu who were both tired out from their journey, all fell fast asleep, so they did not witness what happened when Gwion stoked the fire that one last time. They did not see the mixture boiling over, throwing out three precious drops of liquid that scalded Gwion's thumb. To ease the pain, he thrust the thumb into his mouth and sucked it without even thinking.

At that moment, the cauldron split in two, pouring out the liquid, which burned the grass and poisoned the lake. Gwion, scared that the Goddess would mete out some dire punishment for his accidental stealing of her three precious drops of Awen, ran away as fast as he could, but Ceridwen awoke in a flash, and screaming with rage, she hurtled after him. She was swift of foot and soon caught up, but just when she was about to dig her fingers into his back, he transformed into a fast, running hare and escaped.

The Goddess, however, turned herself into a black greyhound and continued her pursuit. She was hot on his heels and gaining ground until Gwion came to the river where he immediately transformed into a fish, swimming into the depths, but then Ceridwen, who would not be beaten, became an otter and so the chase went on and on.

When the otter was just about to snatch and eat him, Gwion leapt from the water towards the sky and became a bird, flying fast on the wind, but then the Goddess became a hawk with a razor-sharp beak and great talons.

Realizing that he had no other choice, Gwion turned himself into a grain of wheat and fell to the ground to hide in the earth. Alas, it was not to be, for the Goddess turned herself into a hen, picked up that grain of wheat in her beak and promptly swallowed it.

Happy with her victory, Ceridwen went home, but then, the corn seed she had swallowed grew inside her until she gave birth to a child. Still determined to kill Gwion, she put the newborn into a leather bag and threw him into the ocean. Here he remained for nine months, floating on the water, where he was protected, loved and nurtured by the Moon Goddess, who taught him all the songs and stories she knew herself.

Then, one day, a childless fisherman called Elphin, who was very much down on his luck, found that bag and pulled it out of the water. Slitting the leather open with his fisherman's knife, he gazed in awe when a beautiful child, with so much light shining from his brow, leapt from the bag. With every certainty that he had been blessed and that his run of bad luck had ended, Elphin took the baby home to his wife where they fostered and raised him with all the love they could possibly give. The child grew up to be Taliesin Radiant Brow, the greatest Bard that Wales had ever known.

At the end of this story, I decide to pinpoint Yr Wyddfa or Mount Snowdon, as the inspiration for Dinas Affaraon, the shining city of the druid alchemists since it is the highest peak in the Snowdonia range and indeed the whole of Wales. It is also where Arthur and his knights are supposed to lie sleeping in a hidden cave somewhere on its slopes. It is said that he will awaken one day when the land calls him again in a time of need. What wonderful magical images all of this evokes. I am transported through time and imagination into a vivid Celtic Otherworld.

The legend of Taliesin is a tale of transformation, a story

of spiritual inspiration and letting go of everything that has been outgrown or no longer serves, so that individual life may become a true expression of the Self. Gwion's eventual rebirth into the great Bard Taliesin, provides a suitable metaphor for anyone seeking to awaken their inner creative spark.

After four days in Bala, we continue our journey, spending two nights in Betws-y-Coed, where we visit its Faery Glen. I am not quite sure how I am going to clamber down there really, since the path meanders through a ravine and my left knee has been showing signs of wear and tear for about a year now. I decide to follow my intuition and give it a go since it is a warm sunny day, and I can take my time.

We discover that it is well worth the effort of a slow descent, clinging on to vines and trees where the steps disappear. There is a stunning light effect within the glen itself evoking the image of nature spirits. It is the way those sunbeams filter through the trees on to foaming running water, creating a magical atmosphere that takes me back to the faery pictures and stories I loved long ago.

I sincerely believe that children can benefit from this magic since they are a part of its innocence and wonder, and that keeping it alive in any art form is healthy, life affirming, yet relaxing. There is nothing wrong with creating beautiful images of nature spirits to depict the life force that grows and maintains the natural world around us. Imagination like this, does not prohibit children from pursuing an interest or a future career in the sciences. On the contrary, it can help to foster a more altruistic attitude from which knowledge can grow and prosper for the benefit of all. With our wisdom minds and our heart's love, then, we might begin to create a beautiful energetic world, through our art, our systems, our science.

I heard a spokesperson from the National Trust on television the other day, commenting on how children are spending less and less time outdoors. She observed that when people feel unconnected to something, then they never think about caring for it. It is important that we make a firm connection and commitment to our Earth, that we teach our children to do likewise.

As a child growing up in a working-class family with limited financial and material resources, I was still lucky enough to be able to spend a great deal of time outdoors, being energized and taught by nature. Although I cannot say that I ever saw a faery, I secretly believed in their existence. In my late teens, I also met a young man who was very certain he had seen one in a sunbeam when he was small.

The Faery Glen feels like a very feminine place, an abode of the Earth Goddess in all her splendor, blessed with water, light from the Sun God and the green shelter of trees. Sitting in the sunshine here, is peace for the soul. If a faery realm does exist, then this would certainly be the right sort of place to find it.

After Taliesin, the Goddess, and the Faery, we decide it is time to enter the mountain Kingdom of Yr Wyddfa. The weather continues to be pleasant though partly cloudy. We had booked our seats on the Snowdon Mountain Railway at the same time as our hotels, because of the volume of tourists at this time of year. It is well worth the expense of a ticket, if like me, you are unable to manage a six-hour round trip on foot. My husband is interested in the train, but I am going in search of a hint of the Otherworld city of Dinas Affaraon and those druid alchemists.

The steady climb and the rhythmic shunt of the engine become a part of the landscape experience, as the green valleys, rocky escarpments, lower peaks, and deep lakes come into view and then fall away as we climb higher. There are so many people on foot, such as seasoned hikers, families with children, dog walkers. I experience a momentary pang of regret for not doing this walk when I was younger, but I quickly pull myself back into the moment. I don't want to miss anything by brooding about something I cannot change, so I keep an eye out for King

Arthur's cave instead.

We arrive at the little station on Yr Wyddfa's summit, without locating the sleeping place of the once and future King. If such a cave exists, it is in a Celtic Otherworld that can only be reached beyond the imagination, through the gateway of intuitive mind. As we leave the train, I know that I have less than an hour, only a short time to experience this incredible mountain, so I decide to leave Arthur and his Knights to slumber on.

My husband decides he wants coffee before venturing outside, so we agree to meet up in 15 minutes, as I head off to the summit with my notebook for recording inspiration and my phone for taking photographs. It is spellbinding up here at the top of Wales. The breeze, though fresh, is far from cold. The enormous vista and the sky rolling with white and silvery cloud gives me an uncanny feeling of space, even though there is quite a crowd up here, climbing towards the Cairn, talking about the view or taking pictures. It is almost as if they are ghosts in a mist. As their voices fade from my consciousness, it is as though I have come here alone.

I feel my feet connected to the summit, grounded, and my head connected to the sky where lone birds rise and fall on wind currents. I take three good breaths of pure mountain air and know instinctively that this is a thin place, a threshold place. In my mind's eye, I have a sudden image of a white star shining way above my head, so any truth in a legend of druid alchemists seems much more plausible. At the same time, I find myself thinking more about Merlin than Arthur. There are words carved into the rock face outside the café proclaiming the summit of Yr Wyddfa to be closer to heaven, and why not? I am still getting that star image.

My husband joins me outside and we lean on a wall to look out over the Kingdom of Eryri spreading out below, all lit by the impression of a star over the mountain. I cannot see Dinas Affaraon, but I feel sure that it must be somewhere not far from here, close to where Arthur lies sleeping, through that intuitive gateway and on through the mists of imagination and dreams.

Inspiration starts flowing, so I begin scribbling a first draft of the poem that heads this chapter. Task complete, I reluctantly detach from this magical place, and turn myself back into a tourist so we can catch our return ride to the visitor's center in Llanberis. We sit in the little steam train, still feeling a little overawed, our minds quietened by the mountain. However, once back in Llanberis we talk about how we still have a fine half day in which to enjoy a leisurely stroll around the village of Beddgelert and the last night of our holiday, at a hotel called the Royal Goat, where we plan to celebrate this wonderful week in Snowdonia with a good dinner and a glass of rosé wine. Tomorrow, we will make our way home, stopping for lunch and taking in the beautiful countryside of Mid Wales.

Practice

Seek out a landscape with a story that appeals to you, somewhere that feels resonant with your own life. Perhaps you have found a suitable historical or beauty spot in your local area, or maybe you would prefer a holiday destination. You may even be able to plan a pilgrimage to a site that you have always wanted to visit at home or abroad. Wherever you choose to do this exercise, record your impressions so that you can use your own art form to both describe and celebrate your connection and understanding.

Taliesin appeals to me because I am a poet with a Celtic heart. The stories of King Arthur, Merlin and the Otherworldly Priestesses resonate, because I love their mysticism and magic. The quest for the Holy Grail, is especially significant, because it spins rainbow threads from which I can weave my art and spiritual life into a single tapestry.

Chapter Fifteen

A Thread of Arthurian Magic

Springtime Twilight
The far horizon
is muted pink roses
and smoky amethysts
over ice blue seas
white gulls sail silent
in softer hued skies
of aquamarine silk
as earth slows down
to a blackbird's song
of springtime twilight.
Iona Jenkins

There is something magical about islands, something which never fails to ignite my imagination. Whenever I wake at sunrise, and stand on my balcony looking towards the south, I can see the islands of Steep Holm and Flat Holm, floating in the mists of Môr Hafren/Bristol Channel. My Welsh husband informs me that Môr Hafren means Severn Sea, and that is exactly what this stretch of water feels like to me. The name Bristol Channel doesn't resonate in quite the same way because it sounds more urban or industrial. The Welsh language again sounds more poetic, evocative and in keeping with what I am about to relate.

Throughout the day, the appearance of the islands changes with the position of the sun, the movement of clouds and the color of the sea reflecting the sky above it. Across the water from my apartment in Wales (Cymru), lie the West Country shores of England (Lloegr) and the county of Somerset, where at night, electric lights twinkle in tune with the stars. Beyond the islands, the Welsh coastline veers around to the west, where Môr Hafren eventually flows out into the Celtic Sea and the wider Atlantic Ocean beyond.

The two islands are often a focus through which to open that golden door. Whatever the time of day, whatever the season, I sometimes find myself looking out over an ancient Celtic kingdom, that extends through my stretch of Severn Sea and the land on either side of it. I become more aware of headlands, hills, islands, and green spaces, as today's seaside towns fall out of focus. The spirit of a time long past takes over, as my inner vision decides what is more important to the artist.

I cannot see Glastonbury from my balcony, but if I look beyond the islands of Steep Holm and Flat Holm, I can make out the seafront of a small town called Burnham-on-Sea. Driving from Wales into England, by car, it is not far from here that our journey turns away from the coast into the green picturesque, Somerset countryside. Approaching Glastonbury, we are then greeted by the sight of the Tor with its tower, rising above the Somerset levels, an area prone to flooding. It has been said, that once, the area around Glastonbury was surrounded by water and that it was known as the Isle of Avalon, legendary home of the priestesses who served the Goddess of the Land. Soon I begin to see my Celtic Kingdom as more of an archipelago, as the legend adds a little substance to my creative vision.

On my small outside space in Penarth, my mind is making connections between word and myth. PEN in Welsh means head and ARTH means bear. From ARTH comes the name ARTHUR. King Arthur was often associated with the bear totem and legend also tells that he was taken by boat to the priestesses of Avalon to be healed of his wounds. This, of course, fits in very well with my idea of an ancient Celtic Kingdom linked to tales of the Once and Future King. At this point, I could think about writing a poem or plotting a story, but instead I decide to do an Internet search. I have never seen any reference to King Arthur relating to this area, so I would like to find out whether there is any small link, be it factual or legendary, which might fit any of my intuitive feelings and images.

Sadly, I soon discover that there is no solid evidence of an actual King Arthur, so maybe he is only a dream, a tale told around campfires by the Druid bards of old. However, Wales Online has information suggesting if he ever did exist, then he was likely to have been Welsh, with strong links to Brittany in France. There is also an idea that Arthurian legends spring from snippets of tales traceable to 7th century Wales. If those ideas were proved correct, then there might at least be a link to those Welsh bards of old. However, the English and Scots also have their own claims on King Arthur.

In the 12th century, Anglo-Norman cleric, and historian Geoffrey of Monmouth, famous for making the Arthurian tales popular, declared the Roman fortress town of Caerleon in the Welsh county of Monmouthshire to be the site of King Arthur's Court or Camelot. Since there was no Internet in Geoffrey's time and no real evidence to back up his claims, his ideas are thought to be fantasy not history. However, something had fired his imagination, so I make a note to go there and check it out as a possible source of inspiration.

More recently, there have been discoveries of metalwork in the excavation of a hill fort at a site in Dinas Powis, a village about two miles from my home. This site, once occupied between the 5th and 7th centuries, appears to have enjoyed high status, like Cadbury Castle in Somerset and Tintagel in Cornwall, both of which have their own strong Arthurian stories.

According to Wales Online again, Welsh cleric, Caradoc of Llancarfan in the Vale of Glamorgan, was the first writer to associate King Arthur with Glastonbury when he penned a version of the kidnapping of Queen Guinevere, in his *Vitae Gildas*, for some Christian monks in Glastonbury. There is, after all, a historical connection between the Vale of Glamorgan and

Glastonbury, albeit a Christian one with an interest in legend.

It seems to me that such legends of Arthur form a link between ancient Celtic spirituality in Britain and the later Christian one which arrived with the Roman occupation. Jesus had twelve disciples and Arthur had twelve knights, the legendary Holy Grail became synonymous with the chalice cup of the last supper. It is likely, the early Celtic Christians would have blended their new faith with the native Druidry of that era. This is not difficult to understand. In a former role as a secondary school counsellor, it came to my notice how easily some Peruvian families blended Spanish Catholicism with elements of their birth country's native Inca shamanism, the spirituality of their early ancestors. Like Druidry, this wisdom has likely survived by being allowed to grow and evolve into a contemporary form.

A convenient resting place has been made in the grounds of Glastonbury Abbey for bones supposed to be the remains of King Arthur and his Queen Guinevere. Some believe this abbey was founded by Joseph of Arimathea, a relative of Jesus Christ. This legend, tells of Joseph, traveling to Britain, with Mary. Whether it was Mary the mother of Christ or Mary Magdalene remains uncertain. Either way, the travelers are reputed to have brought a cup, or cruets containing the blood and sweat of Jesus Christ on the cross, to Glastonbury. Here we have a Christian story blending with the native Arthurian legend of the Holy Grail. Whatever their faith or belief, Glastonbury, like the labyrinth, meets all seekers and pilgrims where they are, and there is always something for everybody since the real experience starts within.

I conclude that my ancient Celtic kingdom not only exists in my inner world with its links to Arthurian and Christian legend, but, that the spirit or angel of this place, the energy holding it all together, could also be relating a tale, from a memory held by the landscape outside my window. This is a story that might have its origins in a tiny historical grain of truth, based on a local 7th century King. Arthur has also been associated with the bright star Arcturus, the guardian of the great bear. It seems that the legends of Arthur are really tales of an Otherworldly Avatar, an Archangel Michael or even a Celtic Christ, the Once and Future King who comes in spirit to save the land during times of great danger.

I have found neither legend nor factual possibility relating to Queen Guinevere in my area, though she does have that supposed burial site alongside Arthur in Glastonbury Abbey. These powerful female characters, in the form of a worldly queen and nine otherworldly priestesses, have established links with Glastonbury rather than South Wales.

The Arthurian legends are linked to several other places in Wales as well as southwest England and Brittany in northwest France, as their substance exists in the Otherworld, the inner landscapes of the intuitive mind, and again this is where we find the magic. The land speaks to us through our senses in the symbolic and creative language of angels, the flowing spirit of Awen. Perhaps we are all searching for our own idea of the Grail on some level, whether we are aware of it or not.

But what of Merlin? Where is the wise magician, the King's advisor? After all, Merlin's Enclosure or Clas Myrddin is a name for the British Isles. I search for historical or legendary links to an actual court advisor or Arch Druid who might have been the inspiration for the mysterious Merlin. Again, I found none either in the Cardiff area or Vale of Glamorgan. However, searching further west into South Wales, I come across information about a real tree, known as Merlin's oak, that used to stand in the center of Carmarthen (Caerfyrddin in Welsh), also easily accessible from the M4 motorway.

A tale grew up that Merlin had put a curse on this tree and that Carmarthen would fall or drown if it was ever cut down. It was in fact removed when someone set fire to it at the end of the

1970s, and in keeping with the legend, Carmarthen was severely flooded soon after. *The Black Book of Carmarthen*, a manuscript written in Welsh around 1250, includes poems about Merlin and Arthur. The wizard's birthplace could have been a cave on Merlin's Hill (Bryn Myrddin). There is then, the former presence of a real oak tree and *The Black Book*, which is still available in publication, as well as local legend that connects Merlin with Carmarthen.

In Welsh story, the location of Merlin's final resting place is Bardsey Island, which lies just off the southern tip of the Llyn Peninsula on the North Wales coast. The King's advisor is said to inhabit an otherworldly glass tower, surrounded by the thirteen treasures of Britain and attended by nine bards. Since Bardsey Island or Ynys Enlli is also a Celtic Christian site, it too forms a connection between Arthurian legend and early Christianity.

Merlin, creator of dreams, mediator between the internal world of soul and imagination with the outer world of form, relays messages from the Otherworld in symbols. Merlin, then as the magician, plays an important part as an archetype in my own genre of creative work. As a writer, I often work with symbolic images, though they may relate to actual places, objects or living beings in the outer world of form.

Negotiating this inner visionary world of symbols and learning to interpret it has been an important part of learning to walk my own creative path. It could be likened to what a shaman might term walking between worlds. This has arisen easily from my former career background in counselling, psychotherapy and hypnotherapy, and it has almost certainly brought me a stream of inspiration linked to my first attempt at writing a fantasy novel about a quest taking place on a tiny world existing in another dimension. The idea was seeded after contemplating the statue of a white unicorn, its head framed by the branches of trees growing behind the perimeter wall of London's Kew Gardens, on which it has reclined for many years. The unicorn gives an impression of being strategically placed to guard the locked door below it. The seed sown by this statue with its head in the trees eventually grew into my first writing project.

So now, I return to my vision of the Celtic World outside my window, for which I have an idea of a King, whose power and leadership protects, draws together its resources and brings stability. There is the possibility of a worldly Queen in Glastonbury who symbolizes harmony, plenty, growth and safety in the land. The King is advised by a druid magician who interprets and imparts wisdom from his connection to the power of an otherworldly divine feminine in the form of the Priestesses of Avalon who initiate, heal, empower and transmit spiritual inspiration. There is equality between male and female, the powers are balanced. In death, Arthur is said to have passed into the Otherworld where he will remain in the keeping of the High Priestess Morgan, until such times as he is called back to the land. I am listening to the sound of Awen in the waves, the breeze and the birdsong, the angel, speaking through the Creative Spirit of a modern bard, the artist in my own heart.

Content with my exploration of land and legends, I return to my chair on the balcony, where I can look out towards the east and the south. I can enjoy sitting in sunshine until it disappears around 3:30pm on a summer afternoon. The sunrise casts its path of golden light, and the noonday sun sets the sea sparkling with a million diamonds. I cannot watch the sun fall below the horizon as the west is hidden from view by houses along the cliff, but I can watch the rosy glow creeping in over the islands to paint the sky in hues of coral, crimson, smoky amethyst and dove grey.

The landscape changes color and mood as the day progresses, flooding my imagination with words and ideas. Time can illuminate patterns located in the past, the present or occasionally spin threads that flow into the future. Sometimes this landscape is a Celtic Otherworld, a reflection of its spiritual existence, a central golden thread magically woven to connect me into the whole fabric of its life. That is what these rippling waves and floating islands suggest to me, it is the Angels singing creation into being and that is how the symbolic world of my imagination comes to life.

First, I am connected to the landscape around me, to the spirit of place, the angelic stream of creative energy that forms and maintains it. Next the images and words begin to flow around it like the incoming tide, causing poetry, prose or characters that play out a story, to arise like spray flying from the waves. This is the way of the bard or spiritual artist whose purpose is to catch you in an enchanted web of dreams, to entertain, to awaken wonder and awareness of your own creative possibility, so that you may become inspired enough to shine your hidden light out into the world of form.

The sparkling stars in the sky reflect the wisdom inside. If you link to the sunrise, it may fill you with energy and life force. The moon may take you through a silver white door into the realms of the unconscious and awaken intuition. The fertile earth both grounds and nourishes you. Everything that shines, grows and sustains reflects a peaceful fertile Otherworld and its essence will befriend anyone who approaches it with respect and a good heart.

Today, I can really feel the arrival of spring in my whole being as I relax in my garden chair. The tide is high and the water greyish blue, reflecting the sky. The breeze and the waves are soft sighing in perfect harmony, when I decide to increase my connection in meditation.

I notice the tension in my neck and shoulders as I begin to concentrate on the wave and the wind sounds, but then I stop, because the effort of concentration feels inflexible. Instead, I breathe deeply three times, allowing the sounds to flow through me, washing away control, softening my shoulders and eventually all the muscles right down to my feet. As soon as I am completely relaxed, a lone bird pipes a song before I become aware of several more distant birds joining in a background chorus.

The blue of the sky envelops me, as in my imagination I fly like the feathered gull wild and free, flashing through sunlight, floating on air currents, surveying my magic kingdom from above. It is abundant and vibrant, clothed in the elemental colors of earth, water, air and heartwarming fire from the life-giving sun. I watch, as my Kingdom seems to expand across Môr Hafren into Loegr, through the county of Somerset into Wiltshire then back down the Somerset coast into Devon and Cornwall, before sailing over water into the French province of Brittany. Behind me, the land stretches up the West Coast of Wales to the Gower with its sacred wells, Snowdonia, the Llyn Peninsula, Ynys Môn, the druid Isle of Anglesey and across the sea to Ireland, then further north to Iona and the Scottish Isles.

There is a glorious feeling of freedom as I let my imagination circle again and again before my consciousness returns to Môr Hafren, over my two floating islands, finally coming to rest in the garden chair on my balcony. I take another three good breaths of salty air, becoming aware of my feet bringing the rest of my body into solid focus. Once grounded, I remember to close the experience by drawing my usual imaginary curtain, so the veil once again separates the inner and outer landscapes. I am relaxed and totally at peace out here, with the gentle rolling sea and the budding trees on the cliff edge. I decide to practice this meditation again on a warm night, once the season changes, in the hope that I might hitch a ride as far as the summer stars.

Practice

Sit in your chosen place to tune into the landscape. Take three good breaths, relax and allow your mind to become quiet. You may do this exercise with eyes closed, or open as you wish. Some may find it easier to connect by acknowledging and thinking about an Angel of Place, before trying to broaden the experience.

When you feel connected to your Kingdom, then be still and just let the impressions flow, as you begin to communicate with the landscape and/or your interpretation of the Angel of Place. If you receive any legendary or historical associations, you can try looking them up later to see if the impressions you are receiving contain any grain of truth.

If they do not, then something new is seeding in the inner planes of imagination. Use whatever creative medium you prefer, when new life shoots from the seeds that you planted in the womb of the sacred feminine, birth into the world of form to be nurtured and grown in the sunlight.

Chapter Sixteen

A Garden at the Heart of the Universe

Shores of Dawn
In the deep blue of sapphires
tinting the skies beyond sunset
the light of golden stars aflame
upon the calm of summer seas
and all around I hear the sound
a soft chorale, harmonic flows
from gardens on the shores of dawn.
Iona Jenkins

At the dawning of this book, a new door had opened, and as this leg of my creative spiritual journey is nearing completion, the next door may soon open to another path with all its joys, encounters and challenges. As always, I intend to celebrate both an ending and a new beginning but then out of the blue, a memory of *Bilbo Baggins* in Tolkien's *Lord of the Rings*, as he sets out on his travels singing of a road leading on from his door. A lightning bolt of inspiration, in the moment from an old Hobbit in one of my favorite epics of all time. I take up my pen to create a suitable door for my next project.

A new door has opened
And the road meanders on
as I stand on the threshold
at the dawn of my journey
birds flutter in hedgerows
and delicate silvered webs
sparkle with drops of water
on the dew drenched green

wild scented with flowers.

Looking down my present road, I catch a vision of a garden in the mists of morning. There is something so magical about gardens and perhaps magic is what happens, when man works in direct cooperation with the Creative Spirit to produce a beautiful living environment, changing color and form in a seasonal kaleidoscope. Gardens have individual atmospheres, sometimes even themes. I love walled gardens, because they remind me of *The Secret Garden*, Frances Hodgson-Burnett's classic novel, which touched me deeply in late childhood. Set in my home county of Yorkshire, the story unfolds, as Mary, an orphaned girl, discovers the door to a forgotten, neglected garden and brings it back to life. In doing so, she unleashes the creative, nurturing power of the mother that heals her own sorrow, as well as the pain of her uncle and her cousin Colin.

There are those who love gardening as a creative path, and I am grateful for the dedication these people show for their own journey, for I love to sit in their masterpieces, as much as I love to sit in the Sistine Chapel amongst the sacred art of Michelangelo. All of it is born from heart-centered cooperation and effort.

Green spaces are therapeutic. They are also essential to urban folk since they link us not only to the earth, but also to the soul of the land. Without green, human beings would live soul-less lives. Green is a must for maintaining mental, emotional, and physical health in city children and adolescents, as well as adults, who lead busy stressful lives amongst the tightly packed buildings, dense traffic, hard concrete and tarmac.

I began writing poetry many years ago in Yorkshire, during a very difficult emotional time, following the breakup of my first marriage. It was, however, the decision to accept a teaching post on the outskirts of London that acted as a catalyst for the profound healing and changes that would eventually turn me into a regular poet.

Two years on, after marrying for the second time I settled with my new husband in West London, discovering the magic of many green spaces along the River Thames and especially Kew Gardens. This is where I really became aware of just how much inspiration came flowing towards me from the natural world, where my true path became visible, and the journey turned into a real experience. I felt as though I had awoken from a deep sleep, as I began to participate in the wonder of my own life again.

It was like diving into a river to be carried along in its bubbling melody. It was like flying in the wind, rustling through summer leaves, then lying on green earth, flower scented and lulled into a dream by the warmth of honey golden sunlight. I saw the elements that form the world, mingling and singing their choral harmony in the Great Song that anyone can hear by simply being and experiencing, instead of thinking and analyzing all the time. Memories of long-forgotten skills came back to me.

The road eventually took us on from West London to the Vale of Glamorgan in South Wales and a small seaside town, which coincidentally is sometimes called the Garden by the Sea. Here, the stream widened, its inspiration flowing in across new Celtic landscapes, over the sea in waves that wash the pebbled shores below the cliff outside my home. Sitting on the headland, looking across Môr Hafren, at the Somerset coast, I found my connection to Glastonbury again and to Chalice Well, which is situated between the Tor and Chalice Hill in one of the most beautiful gardens I have ever visited. This is a truly sacred place, a peaceful sanctuary, where the veil thins into an easy awareness of more subtle dimensions.

The Well and its surrounding gardens are cared for and tended by the Chalice Well Trust, a charity founded in 1959 by Wellesley Tudor Pole, who wanted to preserve them for the benefit of all. The site is both a meeting place and a sanctuary for people of all beliefs and faiths that transcends all differences in its acknowledgement of common sacred space.

Chalice Well, like my angel guide, speaks to me through the heart. Entering the site through a walkway of flowers, the noise of the world quickly falls away, as the gentle atmosphere wraps me in its cloak of peace. This is a dream of ancient Avalon, a sacred, powerful feminine place, nurturing, healing and protective like the arms of the Goddess, the Divine Mother. It was here that I became aware of what I can only describe as angelic presence all around me.

On that day the garden seemed to be inhabited by a crowd of gentle white light beings, whose ethereal images lit up my imagination. Those images misted away as soon as I closed the exit gate and returned to my hotel, but then to my surprise, they were there once more, as soon as I retired, surrounding me with their light until I fell asleep. In the morning they were gone again, but I had seen what I was meant to see.

It is wonderful how visitors respect the peace in that garden. There are usually people meditating on the steps, on the low wall around the well, or sitting in an area known as the Sanctuary, with its stone altar, votive candles and beautiful rustic statue of a Madonna and Child. It doesn't matter whether you call her Mary, Isis, Brighid or any other name that originates from whatever religion or philosophy you are happy with. The blessing of this sacred feminine place will almost certainly touch your heart. The Creative Spirit does not belong exclusively to any one faith, it belongs to all. We are not separate, for separation is only an illusion we have chosen to create. The amazing sacred art, architecture, crafts, poetry, stories, music, prayers, ceremonies and celebrations found in both contemporary and tribal cultures throughout the world bear witness to that. We started painting at the dawn of human civilization, when we lived in caves.

According to the Chalice Well Trust guide booklet, the water which is reddish from a high iron content, flows out of the earth below Glastonbury Tor, but its actual source remains unknown. It might come from deep within the earth, more immediately from underneath the Tor, or according to some, from further afield, perhaps even the mountains of Wales. Legend says that the water turned red when Joseph of Arimathea buried those two cruets or a cup containing blood and water from Christ's wounds somewhere under Chalice Hill. The site around Glastonbury Tor and Chalice Well, then, is where the Arthurian Grail legend and the Cup of Christ flow together in southwest England like the stream that feeds the well.

I became a companion of Chalice Well, in the same way as I became a Friend of Kew Gardens, because I wanted to make my own small contribution towards the preservation of this site. Every year, the Trust holds a Companion's Day, when we all meet in the garden to celebrate and to explore different spiritual philosophies through talks, activities, and lunch together. In addition to Companion's Day, there is also a week of workshops and events dedicated to exploring the philosophy chosen for that year.

Chalice Well has its own small shop with a bright atmosphere, selling good quality spiritual books, CDs, crystals, jewelry, rugs, cards, meditation tools and Chalice Well Essences. I love these vibrational plant essences, because they are made using the Chalice Well waters and plants from the surrounding garden, where I have so often found my own magic. We are all different and I realize plant and flower essences may not be for everyone. It is up to each artist to discover their own personal healing tools, sacred objects, and useful resources, as part of their personal quest to find healing and creative wisdom on the path.

Chalice Well is like the garden of my heart on Earth, a sacred space where man's spiritual aspirations and artistic drive have led to cooperation with the Creative Spirit in the making of an incredible retreat where all are welcome, regardless of creed or culture. Here the angels whisper their language of inspiration and wisdom, in tune with the stream of healing waters that runs through the veins of Mother Earth. A short walk away, the masculine Tor rises towards the heavens with Saint Michael's Tower at the summit, like a sword of truth pointing towards the sky, or Merlin's wand drawing light down into the well.

Returning home, it is already early afternoon, when I take time out to sit in silence and enjoy the view from my balcony again. Today, the sea rolls in with a vision of another garden somewhere way beyond the horizon and through the summer stars. I am content with this image, though not surprised since a garden, in my opinion, is always a positive fertile place to begin or end any journey, as it both soothes the soul and energizes the body. Although today's vision is spontaneous, I have the impression that anyone wishing to locate the entrance to this peaceful sanctuary at the heart of the universe in themselves, might find their quest easier in the dawn time, when the sun, moon and stars all share the same sky.

Meditating on my vision, I enter the mystery through an archway, set in grey stone walls, where thick swathes of wisteria tumble down like pale waterfalls of amethyst and pink-tinged white. This garden is alive with fresh green growth, rainbows of spring flowers, fruit trees heavy with blossoms and bright bees gathering pollen, in springtime perfumes all heaven scented.

The ivory marble statue of a goddess wearing a gown fashioned in Grecian or possibly Roman style, holding a jug in one hand and a chalice cup in the other, comes alive with the kiss of a single sunbeam. Her hair curled and piled upon her head shines reddish gold, whilst her complexion, pale as the moon, is enhanced by a light rosy glow that sets off the white silken folds of her garment, belted with a cord of plaited gold and silver threads. Before her, a carved stone pillar stands upon the earth, whilst all around, devas tending the garden are gathering with all other manner of angels, ethereal and transparent in white light. The lady places the once marble jug, which has now turned silver, down upon the grass. At that moment, I am surprised to see my own angel guide appear behind her. The miraculous jug soon begins to fill up with a substance, reminiscent of liquid honey.

"ASTARIEL."

A light breeze sighs the angel's name through the apple blossom. There is wisdom in this garden, as well as inspiration, healing, bright magic, and blessings in abundance.

"Will you not drink of life's sweetness?" the Goddess invites me.

I have an impression that she and the angel are working together in the Presence that has sung this garden into being. I experience both clarity of mind and lightness of being, dreaming in this rare sunlit place. I am aware too, of a gentle warmth stroking the crown of my head, as she pours golden elixir from the jug into the opalescent white chalice cup, which all at once begins to glow with pale colors that form impressions of flowers flowing through it.

"Will you not drink?" she repeats, her eyes reflecting the cornflower blue that paints the sky when she places the cup upon the pillar of carved stone.

"If this cup is the sweetness of life, then I shall be happy to drink from it, for I have often grown weary in the waves of bitter experience that have washed up not only upon my own shores, but also upon the shores of the world."

"Then drink." There is real compassion in those eyes.

The goddess sheds a single tear that splashes down to water the earth around her feet, where all at once, a white flower shaped like a star, springs up and becomes another reflection in the chalice.

I take her cup and sip the golden elixir, savoring the healing warmth and sweetness of a thousand flowers that seems to infuse my whole being with life and light. When the cup is finally empty, I offer it back to her, but she shakes her head smiling.

"Will you not keep my cup?" she says. "This vessel has been fashioned with you in mind and if you leave it here, on the stone pillar, it will fill right up to the brim with golden elixir, every morning at sunrise whether or not you are awake. All you need to do upon rising, is to remember my garden and the cup will present itself according to your needs. Over time, you may discover your life changing for the better with your vitality increasing to enhance your health, mood and inspiration."

"Thank you for your kindness and compassion," I reply. "I will accept your gift, for this vessel of life's sweetness has both revived me and answered some questions."

As I replace my own cup upon the pillar, the goddess is already resuming the form of a marble statue, whilst the white light beings go about their business of tending to the plants and trees or return to whatever tasks they are assigned. Only the angel Astariel remains.

"You are always welcome here," the angel tells me, leaning forward to take hold of both my hands. "The wheel of the year turns, dreams come and go, but sweetness is eternal in the Garden at the Heart of the Universe."

And with those words, both my angel, who I may now call Astariel, and the garden dissolve into mist, and I am sitting by my open door again, looking across Môr Hafren towards the Somerset coast, listening to sweet waves lapping over the shore, the gulls calling and the spring green leaves rustling on the cliff.

Beyond all notions of right and wrong is a garden. I'll meet you there.
Rumi

Practice

Write the word *Garden* in the middle of a blank page, take three breaths, and gently focus on your heart space. When you feel relaxed and calm, write down all the different sensory memories and threads of inspiration that flow as you start to tune into the idea of an inner secret garden.

If you have a garden in the outer world, or a place to plant pots, then you could do some work with that space, using any ideas that you received from the above exercise. Gardens provide us with soul balm and sanctuary, they are an amazing source of both spiritual and artistic inspiration.

As an alternative, you may prefer to connect to a garden or two by visiting one that is open to the public. A National Trust membership gives access to the most beautiful grounds all over Britain. Chalice Well in Glastonbury has its own Companions membership, which allows free entrance. For non-members, there is a modest entry fee.

If it feels right for you, then you could also use meditation to link up with your own Garden at the heart of the Universe.

Finally, do you find that gardens help you with your own art, and if so, what sort of inspiration do you receive from them? In addition to artistic impressions, record any ideas or messages that might help you to grow spiritually. These two strands often flow together like the winding patterns of Celtic knotwork, or the plaited silver and gold threads of the belt worn by the Goddess I described in my own garden.

Chapter Seventeen

Astariel

Flower Moon

A spring full moon, a super moon
for blossom time and May bloom
white winged birds all soaring free
over golden waves across the sea
earth and sky merging in twilight
illuminated dreams in flower light
of pastel shades on soft pearl white
when glittering stars begin to rise
and indigo curtains deep but bright
are draped upon the shores of night
Iona Jenkins

This May full moon, known as the Flower Moon, is also a supermoon, because its appearance is larger than usual. Rising round and pale above the ocean on a twilight background of pink grey and aqua, she grows brighter, as the sky deepens to royal blue and finally indigo. The Flower Moon is now a magnificent orb of vibrant yellow, reflecting her light over the ocean as a path of molten gold that stretches between the coasts of Wales and Somerset. Eventually, when the light changes again to silver white, the shining path expands growing wider and wider, bright and visible through gaps between the leaves of springtime trees, where it shimmers and ripples below the cliff like dancing silver sprites.

The Flower Goddess has poured her elixir of light upon the fertile earth, which will burst into a feast of scented color and life when the sun rises, with blossoms and flowering plants covering every green space. This is my favorite time of year, when the incredible beauty outside fills my senses and moves my pen across the paper in bursts of enthusiastic inspiration. Winter worries are dissolving, as my soul drinks from a chalice of sunlight and flowers. I am creating with the angels, all singing this incredible green life into being.

And where the full moon shines, there also, I find Astariel, dancing with the Goddess in a stream of Awen, guiding me to translate their symbols into the words and concepts that form this book.

"Astariel."

As soon as I call that name, an inner sense of hearing picks up the song of a breeze whispering through apple blossoms in my dreaming garden that lies beyond the horizon and through the summer stars. The Flower Moon, reflecting on the water, brings me a strong inclination to write, as soon I see the white angel light in my mind's eye shimmering with pastel colors like a beautiful opal. Tonight, there are images of flowers in the light that remind me of the chalice in that garden at the heart of the universe.

"Astariel," I whisper again, "I see that you have brought me flowers."

"That is because your awareness is illuminated by an exceptionally bright Flower Moon. You are open to new ideas and energy from the abundance and growth of this spring season, are you not? I see that you have discovered my name then."

"Yes, I first heard it on a breeze, rustling the apple boughs in the garden of my heart. I have been writing notes for two days now."

"The full moon forms a bridge that connects you to the Creative Spirit. Since the moon influences the tides, then it is fair to say that its influence, on the human body, which contains a high percentage of water, is likely to be substantial. The full moon is not necessarily inspiring for everyone though.

Some may prefer the moon waxing whilst others may like it on the wane. Then again, some people are prone to emotional unbalance and turmoil during this bright phase of the lunar cycle, and of course, there are those who would ignore the moon completely. Let us say that it holds a great deal of possibility for stable human beings of spiritual and/or artistic inclination.

The full moon has been known to increase feelings of anxiety or to stimulate mental and emotional instability since she illuminates repressed shadows in the soul, hiding forgotten in corners of the unconscious mind. This can cause psychic disturbance often referred to as lunacy, and even criminal behavior. Your dark tales of werewolves and vampires have no doubt evolved from this full moon effect. Yet, if challenges posed by the shadow are met, then a full moon's effect can be life enhancing. I would suggest only doing moon meditation when you feel relaxed and stable, but then you already know that don't you?"

"Mmm," I ponder on his words for a minute. "A full moon rising brings me the potential for realization and change. In addition, my creativity receives a rapid boost from bathing in her light. I have gradually learned not to fear the shadows she illuminates, not just because I have useful therapeutic skills, but also because my ability to trust in the wisdom and flow of my life is increasing all the time. This full moon and the February Snow Moon do seem to have a particular potency for me. You, however, are not a shadow and since I often find you in full moonlight, which is often a beautiful, creative time, then you are my wise inspiration."

There is a soft warm feeling, as Astariel places a delicate hand upon my shoulder.

"As I told you when we first spoke, I am your creative wisdom, and yes, you are getting the picture," he says, "though there is yet so much more for you to understand about me and my kind. I have indeed, already, brought you symbolic items from the Archangels of the four directions, illustrated by your Wheel of the Year. From the East and the rising sun, the elixir of Raphael. From the South with the sun at noon, the blue cloak of Michael. From the sunset in the West, a golden harp from Gabriel. From the North and the night sky, I brought you Oriel's lantern of stars to light your way. Finally, the Archangel called Sandalphon, who stands tall upon the Earth at the foot of the Tree of Life, sends you a pair of bronze leather sandals to keep your feet upon the ground. I would consider it wise to visualize wearing them before you do any spiritual journeying since they will always plant you safely back on the earth."

"I am very happy to receive the sandals," I tell him. "They are a wonderful earthy treasure for my imagination to consider. The idea of the other four treasures, as you know, have already inspired me with so many ideas, associations, and words. Now there are five, which evoke a picture of a pentagram or five-pointed star."

Astariel nods in agreement. "Such a symbol is a good way to remember them."

For a moment, Astariel's presence seems to spread throughout the entire room before an image of a great oak with golden leaves slides into my mind. Leaning against the tree, as though he were almost connected to its trunk, I see a coppery bronze image of a very tall slender angel wearing leather sandals. This Archangel belongs to the Earth, but the top of his head is so obviously in the stars. I note that the sandals are important to my sense of well-being. I am reminded of roots going deep into the ground and branches reaching towards the sky above the forest. The image dissolves, as I bring my mind back to the conversation.

"I have just seen the importance of the sandals in a beautiful picture," I tell him, recounting my vision. "We have worked well together, haven't we?"

"I totally agree," Astariel approves, before I continue.

"Yes," I confirm, "and what's more, my work on this book is almost complete. Will you stick around when it's finished?" I ask him. "I've got so used to you being here, especially during a full moon. You have brought so much inspiration into my life."

"And I have been trying to get your attention for years of your earth time. Now, at last, since you are not so busy working, or wading through so many personal problems, you have finally found a way forward, and in doing that, you have actually noticed me." There is laughter in Astariel's eyes, and his tone is mildly teasing.

"I am sorry," I sigh as I answer, staring downcast at the rug on the floor in front of me. "I am aware that I've wasted a lot of creative hours, sometimes years, giving over too much time to things that in retrospect seem much less important than they did previously."

The angel's presence feels both warm and generous as he reassures me. "I cannot say in all honesty I agree with that. You have discovered a creative wisdom path, and it is true to say that even the most painful areas of your life have played a part in bringing you to this point. Nothing has been wasted and I have already told you that time has no importance for me. The most effective change comes from a gradual wearing away, of beliefs and attitudes that are no longer fit for purpose. What I would emphasize, is that you have free will and my presence in your life is a matter of choice. We set no age limit on any artist, so if you are conscious, then inspiration is available to you until your last breath."

"Interesting," I reply. "So, more and more I am becoming convinced that human beings really do form an integral part of the Creative Spirit, albeit at the end of the chain where energy and information unite into form. So, it seems like it all filters down in frequency from the Creative Spirit, like the three bars of light in the Awen symbol shining down from three dots representing the drops of inspiration from Ceridwen's cauldron. Therefore, you, in your more subtle frequency, must be the energy channel above me. What do you have to say about that?" I ask, hoping that he might give me some more information, but what I get is another of his typical wait-and-see replies.

"You appear to have written your way into the beginning of an understanding, from an artist's point of view, but that is not the end of the story, for there is a great deal more for you to explore and experience on your creative path. As I always say, everything happens in its season, and you will understand when the time is right."

"Okay then," I sigh, remembering that he usually prefers me to work things out for myself first. "So maybe it's like one of the images I use all the time," I continue, "a door opens, and a new path calls me. Each leg of this creative journey contains its own challenges, learning and good times, then when it's over, there is always another door. I suppose that much of what happens on future journeys, arises from the choices I make in the present. I enjoy writing, but I also want to take some responsibility for creating a life that's right for me, by living in Awen, listening to the language of angels, so that my future is filled with sweetness from the Garden at the Heart of the Universe. Right now, I have a sense of Creative Spirit in the Sacred Feminine."

"The enjoyment is to be had by embracing every step of the path itself, rather than wondering about journey's end, for that distracts from the synchronicity of the present. And yes, there is always a Goddess in the garden," Astariel says, his eyes brimming with the same sweetness as the chalice that my own Goddess gave to me. "For how can anything be brought into the world of form, if there is no feminine to give birth to it?" he concludes.

"But, Astariel," I add, "just suppose that I had been born into a different background, might not the Goddess present herself in a completely different way?"

"The appearance of a Goddess in your interpretation of

the garden does, of course, contain your own symbolism, originating from those Celtic, Greek and Roman myths with which you are familiar, as well as your genetics," Astariel tells me. "The Divine Feminine/Goddess meets everyone equally, and exactly where they are, in much the same way as a labyrinth or Chalice Well. She reflects the soul like a mirror, an image of the moon on water. The Goddess, the vegetation and the form of the garden might also look different, according to whatever aspect of the feminine is currently flowing through someone's life. Factors such as country of origin, ancestry, education, migration, friendships, spirituality, well-being, for example, may all exert their own measure of influence at any given time. People everywhere are products of their own stories, offering diverse variations on theme and artwork, but in the end, all those stories connect, like your Celtic knotwork, forming into verses of one great ballad or song. The sun, the moon and the stars shine just the same over the entire world."

As soon as this teaching ends my mind is already linking into another idea.

"In addition to bringing me your own kind of inspiration, I see that you also form my link to a whole subtle stream of Awen. You connect me to other angelic beings, who appear in symbolic form like beautiful atmospheric paintings, evoking new feelings and possibilities. A poem I wrote yesterday, reflects the qualities of peace and healing angels that come to me in soft images of long beaches, pale seas and wide skies. I am beginning to sense the existence of a tangible powerful energy behind the word *love*, as my connection to you and others of your kind deepens."

Astariel looks pleased, "Yes, there is in fact a choir responsible for the harmony of a human being, though not everyone either acknowledges or relates to that. Now you, as an artist, are just beginning to hear and to understand something of the force that drives the universe. Do you remember the little stone birdbath that used to sit on the flowering border of your small patio garden, when you lived in London?"

"Why yes," I answer with enthusiasm. "I wanted to buy it as soon as I saw it in the garden center at Syon Park, which also has amazing greenhouses, and a long lake. I once had an image of the moon reflected in the water of that lake, even though it was daylight on a summer's day. I remember sitting on a bench to write, when I noticed an artist sketching on the bank directly opposite me. I caught a scent of white stargazer lilies that seemed to follow me as I walked back towards the entrance to the park. It is as though the park, the lake, and the birdbath, were all a part of that image of the moon on water."

"And do you remember the words that were carved on that birdbath?" he asks smiling.

"Of course," I reply, "a single verse by Dorothy Frances Gurney."

The kiss of the sun for pardon
The song of the birds for mirth
You are nearer God's heart in a garden
than anywhere else on earth.

"So, close your eyes," the angel suggests, "and allow the wings of your imagination to fly you back to the Garden at the Heart of the Universe, then tell me what you see there now."

"I see a white moon in a sky strewn with bright stars. A light breeze rustles the blossoms on the fruit trees. Soon there will be apples shining silver in moonlight, all ripening to gold in the sunrise and reflecting in the chalice, like the morning light reflects on the sea outside my window. An angel being who looks like you, sits playing a golden harp that stands upon the grass and I am aware that this garden is really as vast as my imagination can stretch. I sit beneath a hazel tree where straight away, I see a masculine smiling face forming from a cluster of stars in the sky above and I recall having seen a similar vision before, on a visit I made to Stonehenge many years ago. It is the face of a gentle star, in love with the Goddess in the Garden at the Heart of the Universe. Together they are creative wisdom. This love is not fluffy or sentimental, it is strong and powerful beyond measure."

"Congratulations, I am proud of you. By following all the signs along this path of light, created by the moon from her reflection on water, you have discovered the love in your heart also reflects the Creative Spirit, that builds and drives your inner universe, which in turn reflects the Universe stretching out beyond the planet you live on. You found your way back to the garden," Astariel laughs, floating back towards the sea outside, where he slowly begins to dissolve into the Flower Moon night.

"Thank you, Astariel," I whisper with gratitude, as the last shimmer of his pearl white and pale colors melt back into the flow of ocean and night. I wish he could have stayed a little longer, although deep in my heart, I know that our connection remains strong, and that the angel is only a dream away. I take a minute to breathe deeply, preparing to leave the moon behind and center myself in the world of form, but first, I imagine a pair of bronze leather sandals hugging my feet, connecting me to the ground. Safely back on earth, I head for the kitchen and make myself a mug of red tea for drinking as I finish my notes.

Practice

In this chapter, the angel Astariel suggests that there is always a Goddess in the Garden. He also asks how anything that has been seeded could ever be born into the world of form without the presence of the feminine.

Although she has been much maligned and marginalized by centuries of fear that have included witch hunts, inquisitions, the torture, and abuse of the feminine, the Goddess in whatever guise we might imagine her, has never deserted us. She still appears for me as energetic, wise and nurturing, dancing in equal partnership, to form a balance of power with a true loving vision of a creative masculine God. Together, they make the Universe harmonic. We can see her shining in the four elements, in the light of sun, moon and stars, in our beautiful blue planet, as well as ensouling human art with her radiance.

We in the West are out of balance in our symbolic thinking. We banished Sophia from the Holy Trinity, leaving only her token, the dove. The divine triad became entirely masculine, leaving the divinity of the receptive and creative feminine process outside of it.
Alice O. Howell, *The Dove in the Stone*, p. 93, Quest Books 1988

If you can set a little time aside to reflect upon the idea of the Sacred Feminine for yourself, you may discover that your own creative inspiration has a certain resonance with an impression of one or more archetypal goddesses.

She may have a particular ethnic origin or belong to a specific spiritual or religious faith. Maybe you have already encountered her in myths, legends and scriptures. Perhaps her essence is connected to a planet, a star, or even one of the four elements. Once you begin to get impressions and ideas, you can google the word Goddess to link with several Internet sites that might be able to help you to expand on them.

How do you see the Divine Feminine now, in terms of your own spirituality and/or art? At this stage, if it feels right, you might like to meditate on the Garden at the Heart of the Universe again to locate her in your own creative inner landscape.

Chapter Eighteen

Art and Soul

Oran Mór

On a hot summer's day
when living green earth
lies basking in the peace
of a sunflower sunshine
hedgerow bees buzzing
and hidden bird twitter
then a seagull cries joy
while a robin trills, clear
for the gentle blue sea
and I am melody melting
in wavesplash and airsigh
the Great Song sounding
from the heart of creation
in the language of angels
my hand begins to write.
Iona Jenkins

A creative spiritual path is a celebration of life, a chance to taste the nectar of fulfilment. The development of spiritual intelligence and wisdom does not always require a strict religious practice, for life itself provides magic for our growth. We only need to remember that the underlying message, contained within the teachings, stories and art of all faiths, is love. It is sometimes all too easy for that most important original message to be lost, whenever it becomes buried under piles of individual power plays and struggles, institutional politics, and dogma.

By adhering to the spiritual essence, the original teachings of love in any faith, as well as adding wisdom gained from individual life experience, and our connection to the natural world, it is also possible to compose a personal moral agenda or code of ethics. In doing so, we become independent, creative, and responsible for our own actions. Applying this intent to a meditation practice may inspire ideas that accurately reflect a personal creative life model. This need not be set in stone, however, and since continuous development and evolution changes everyone, it might be wise to factor in enough space to make a few changes, as awareness and understanding increase.

The Universe does not stand still, and back in 1970, we used to describe joining in that dance of change as 'going with the flow.' Although I would always acknowledge the need for a healthy level of willpower and outward focus to live a useful life that gets things done, I also love to relax, to contemplate the sea outside, to listen to the wind, whenever I experience writer's block. Water flows over obstacles in its path or washes them away, and moving air blows the cobwebs from the corners of forgotten dusty rooms.

My own spirituality contains a good measure of both mystical and experiential dimensions, it is primarily nature and art inspired. Combining this formula with my artistic life, certainly influences my creativity, with a tendency to send my path meandering through the heart, to add an ingredient of love into whatever imaginative potion I happen to be brewing. As I walked the first few footsteps of this path, I was writing for myself, but as I progressed only a few steps further, it became clear to me that my work might help others to open their own doors of imagination, and that like a native tracker, I might be able to leave signs pointing towards those doors.

Many years have passed since I first decided to view my journey through life as a sacred quest, so maybe I have been seeking the Holy Grail of Arthurian legend all along. I have certainly covered a lot of mileage, encountered challenges, wandered into dark or desperate places, as well as enjoying life by participating in feasts and celebrations.

One of my greatest privileges on the quest, has been the chance to meet and often befriend people from a variety of ethnic and cultural backgrounds, both in my working life and on my travels. The Creative Spirit has been generous in showing me such a marvelous palette of color, climates, and ideas. I have also found the time to discover and to consider a good deal of wisdom, contained within a variety of spiritual systems, though I did not choose to settle down permanently in any one of the larger organized faiths. By nature, I am not religious since there is something of a gypsy in me that has always needed to maintain my own good measure of free spirit. More and more, however, I am sensing the existence of a universal community of love and light shining through the boundaries of many religions and cultural traditions yet including them all. We are only asked to tune our heartbeat to its rhythm and harmonize with its song.

For me then, this artistic path, evolving from my life experience, has brought inspiration that triggers writing and a sensitivity to color, enabling me to paint in words. I have arrived at this point through meeting life's challenges, through my work in teaching, mentoring, counselling, psychotherapy, and hypnotherapy, through my love of nature and the arts, through travel, relationships, reiki healing, mindfulness, and meditation, in addition to an exploration and comparison, of various spiritual practices.

Eventually, coming to live in Wales awakened an interest in Celtic legend and spirituality, adding new color and depth to my inner landscape. Then, in early 2018, around the time of Imbolc/Candlemas, my path meandered quite naturally into a study of modern Druidry, so perhaps my footsteps were guided by Brighid/St. Bride, Goddess/Saint of poets and healers on her festival. Druidry, a philosophy rather than a religion, can be practiced alongside any faith or none. Here I am feeling sufficient support for my creative heart without losing any of my freedom as an individual. There is total equality between men and women, respect for the body/mind/spirit connection, as well as all life forms, all existences. There is no age discrimination, it blends well with my love of the natural world and is resonant with my poetic and therapeutic backgrounds.

At this stage of my life's journey, a time I have chosen to describe as my elder or wisdom years, I sometimes prefer to experience intuitively before seeking intellectual evidence to back up my findings. I am enjoying a solid feeling of real belonging on this beautiful planet, a feeling of coming home to myself.

In my twenties, I read *Siddhartha*, a novel by Hermann Hesse. In that time of my youth, the writing made some intellectual sense to me, but only recently, after reading the following extract from it, did I feel the author's words with my whole being, as it touched my heart and soul. At last, I understand, just how much this story shares a resonance with the tale of my own life.

"Have you also learned the secret from the river; that there is no such thing as time?"

A bright smile spread over Vasudeva's face, "Yes, Siddhartha,"
he said, "is this what you mean? That the river is everywhere at
the same time, at the source and at the mouth, at the waterfall,
at the ferry, at the current, in the ocean and in the mountains,
everywhere and that the present only exists for it, not the shadow
of the past nor the shadow of the future."
Hermann Hesse, *Siddhartha*, 1922, p. 123, Macmillan Collector's Library edition 2020

My spiritual path with all its life experience has been both varied and eventful, sometimes beautiful, sometimes challenging, occasionally even terrible. Unlike Siddhartha who made a conscious choice, I was forced to leave my place by the River

Thames, take a leap of faith into the water and allow myself to be carried down to the sea. But then, as Hesse suggests, the river is the same everywhere. In my youth, I thought about becoming enlightened, but today such thoughts are rare. All that exists is right here and now in a wholistic experience, where the physical is as sacred as the spiritual, for I no longer see them as separate. I fell into the dream and awoke upon a southwestern shore, where I found my peace in this Flowing Spirit. So now, I am becoming a writer of my own story, enjoying being embodied, connected, relaxed, and inspired on the edge of this threshold place. I continue to watch the ocean and its tides rippling with Awen, a mirror reflecting the sky, creating in each moment with every new vision.

In the magic of dawn and twilight, the spaces between night and day, day and night, the veil seems to lift, as the Otherworld begins to weave its delicate ethereal threads into the fabric of my fertile imagination. At such times, I have often experienced a strange feeling that I am standing in a painting. Since I am a spiritually motivated writer, I am taking as much responsibility as I can for creating my own life. As already indicated in my last conversation with Astariel, I remain dedicated to the notion that humanity forms an integral part of the creative force, both spiritually and materially, which is why I now consider the development of love to be so very important.

The angel realm appears in my internal landscape as a domain of exquisite color and light, where words arise like notes from a celestial ocean breaking in waves of sound and a flurry of bright wings upon the shores of human consciousness. It seems to me that angels work their creative wisdom through sacred feminine energy, in a way that is both nourishing and life enhancing. Astariel is a harmonious blend of opposites, my vision of an angelic being who personifies the Creative Spirit, as I see it in my own humanity. I open a door, to allow the angel who appears, both as a gentle inspiring image in my intuitive mind and as a beautiful light on the ocean outside my window, to step into the world of form through my art.

In our role as planetary custodians, we are required to keep a watchful eye on the direction of our own intentions since we are responsible for what we create. I like to use the image of a bright shining lantern to represent my creative light and this symbol helps me to keep my own path clear. Whatever gender we are born into, we all contain our own mixture of masculine and feminine, energy and information, intuition and intellect, wisdom, and creativity, though achieving alchemy by marrying the two halves together in harmony isn't always easy, because we are human beings, who often fall prey to our layers of conditioning. We become discordant and lose our balance. If the masculine information or intellect is too analytical, power hungry or both, the feminine energy will change to the face of a Dark Goddess bringing chaos, as the Garden is exploited, causing it to wither and die into a wasteland. Eventually another Grail Seeker will appear to begin a new quest for the heart's chalice, to reinstate the Divine Feminine and bring the land back into balance.

Similarly, science and art need not be separate. I have known more than one competent musician who was much inspired by mathematics. A scientist might prefer to explain harmony and balance in terms of mathematical formulae, whereas the artist might prefer to illustrate it with visual symbols such as a cross in a circle with its four equal quadrants, or the Taoist yin/yang symbol. There are, of course, people such as Leonardo Da Vinci and Michelangelo, who were fortunate enough to be able to blend both.

We all need to work according to our gifts and abilities. I must confess that I am not much of a mathematician, but I do have the capacity to work as an intuitive creative writer with an active intellect and enough of a magical child to maintain a sense of wonder every time I watch the rising sun paint the sky in fabulous colors. Modern technology, developed by science enables me to access the world from my desk, enhancing and adding creature comforts to my quality of my life, but it is always art that gives me the passion to live it with soul.

My own feminine requires my mind to be gentle yet strong and discerning, creative with a will to cooperate rather than to control. In short, a poet's mind with heart, like the pottery sun face on my wall. Together they draw in creative wisdom. I came from a hard mining background where tough male superiority was so often the norm. Finding this spiritual haven has required action to soften my hard edges, a great deal of soul searching, a willingness to kick out those old niggling little demons hiding in the shadows of my unconscious and a belief in my own purpose. The process is far from finished, and I am not so sure that it ever will be, but as my journey continues, I am enthusiastic and willing to learn from whatever comes along, since Astariel tells me I can receive inspiration right up until my last breath.

Mulling over the idea forms another connection. What if it is possible to use a last breath inspiration to move on into the next story, when the body falls away? That would be real, creative magic, wouldn't it? Not everyone is awake at the end of life, however, but strengthening our connection to the Creative Spirit might achieve the same purpose. Food for thought, as no one living can ever know for certain what might happen through that final door, but nevertheless, the idea holds some promise of participating in the possibility.

We are just past the Summer Solstice and the weather is glorious, as I sit on my balcony watching several gulls soaring across a pale blue sky. The sea is as calm as a lake, though the tide is going out. During this period of hot temperatures and extended daylight, I am aware how the light has already started receding little by little towards the harvest and Autumn Equinox. At present, however, I am in a celebratory mood, close to the end of a journey through the pages of a book, which in its writing has also enhanced my own understanding of our human connection to the whole of creation.

My journey through life has embraced both the spiritual and the material, I have tried to live my truth through interaction with this beautiful inspiring world rather than in seclusion from it. Today, I find those two aspects blending to a greater degree. I am aware of changes that have taken place in my inner world being reflected on the outside. My spirituality has become essentially creative, with a will to write my life as a poem, a line of philosophy, to sing it as a song, paint it in color and light, to describe it in the language of angels.

Studying for a Master's in Education (Guidance and Counselling) a couple of evenings a week during my teaching years, I had the good fortune to meet a professor who taught me to view my daytime teaching work as an art. From her influence, my ability to motivate adolescents in their learning of a modern language blossomed. I also developed an ability to mentor trainee teachers in a way that not only facilitated a growth in their confidence, but also encouraged the development of an individual creative approach. This, then, is where I first began to explore the idea of life as art. After all, if teaching adolescents or mentoring trainee teachers could be viewed in that way, then why not experiment, apply this concept to as many areas of life as possible. After I changed career, I wove this thread into my counselling and psychotherapy practice, and today, it remains an ongoing, interesting life process.

A mistaken need to control everything usually causes anxiety. In learning to live my life as art, I begin to move beyond this need. Anxiety falls away whenever I recognize any aspect of the power and control tyrant lurking in my forest. Then, newly awakened willpower for good paired with wisdom, creates an intuitive connection to my inner angelic realm, bringing a realization of love, light and cooperation. In such conditions, life connects, flowing with harmony and synchronicity, as the angels heal the psyche's shadow tyrants, persuading them to turn their faces towards the sunrise and temper their energy for use on creative projects.

Creative spirituality, then, is fundamentally experiential and heart centered. Opening to love, we accept all aspects of our life experience as an opportunity to learn, to heal, to grow in courage and wisdom, to create, as we walk through those inner and outer landscapes of light and shade. We participate and cooperate, fashioning our cups from the malleable clay of earth, filling them with light, as we paint our patterns and weave new golden threads into the tapestries of our own stories. In actively working from a creative heart, we grow towards the sky like healthy trees bending in the wind. At sun return, we bud and blossom into beauty producing abundant fruit for our harvest.

In jotting down a list of all that continues to inspire me, I find landscapes, seascapes, skyscapes, myths and legends, travel, the seasons, the elements, individual people and cultures, the Earth's creatures, gardens, flowers, trees, sacred places, sacred objects, arts and crafts, sculpture, fabrics and textures, color, music, theatre, poetry, prose, photography, spiritual writing and workshops, friends, humor, sun, moon, stars, the universe. The miracle of life itself is inspiring.

And so, the wheel of the year turns full circle, as harvest time approaches, bringing a sense of peace and harmony to my inner land. The fruit trees in the Garden at the Heart of the Universe are now laden with apples.

We have walked a little way together through the pages of this book, and as we separate to go our individual ways, I would like to thank you for your company. I wonder if you can see a door appearing out of the mist as we come to the end of this walk. This door is yours to open with love, as soon as you feel ready to track your Creative Spirit, to find your own symbols, patterns, guides, angels, and any other inspiring companions you might chance to meet along the way. Remember to celebrate all your achievements and to make all your helpers most welcome. As for me, I am happy to continue journeying on and on beyond the golden door of my poem that leads to "I Know Not Where?"

In offering this account of my own creative spiritual journey so far, I find myself light flowing in a stream of Awen, as ideas awaken for writing the next phase of my travels into being. I shall paint my footsteps on a path of rose-scented stars, as the angels speak their words of making. Our lives are a poem, a story, a heartfelt tale of earth and sky, a tiny legend recorded in the vast book of humanity, a single note in a Great Song. We can all learn to sing with bards and angels.

Practice

Jot down a list of everything that inspires you. Leave space to add new ideas. You may decide to work on a personal code of ethics or moral code for your own creative life, as a series of numbered points or even a poem. This work could be electronically filed, printed, painted, written in ink with a calligraphy pen. Let your imagination play around with the idea. You could display it on colored or textured paper, even illustrating it with diagrams, paint, or stickers. This is a chance to explore your own ideas of a spiritual and moral code in creative form, so use whatever appeals to you.

In chapter 16, I wrote my new door into being. Imagine and create a door for yourself. Enjoy and celebrate your Creative Spirit with every step.

Grail Quest

The abundant healing chalice
shines from the centre of a rose
that blooms in the golden heart
of a sanctuary you may enter
only with reverence and respect
for here lies the most sacred site
within the whole bright universe.
Let love awaken, guide your steps
upon your path to seek this place
and if you chance to find it then
my friend you will have everything.
Awen
Iona Jenkins

Pronunciation of Welsh Names

Afagddu	*Av-ag-thi*	Son of Ceridwen and Lord Tegid
Awen	*Ah-wen*	Stream of Inspiration or Flowing Spirit
Bala	*Bal-ah*	Village in North Wales on the edge of Lake Bala
Beddgelert	*Beth-gel-ert*	Village in North Wales
Betws-y-Coed	*Bet-uhs-uh-Coyd*	Village in North Wales with a faery glen
Caer	*Cayer*	A castle or fort
Caerfyrddin	*Cayer-vur-thin*	Carmarthen, a town with a castle in West Wales
Ceridwen	*Kerr-id-wen*	Welsh Goddess in the Taliesin legend
Clas Myrddin	*Clas Mer-thin*	Merlin's Enclosure, the British Isles
Creirwy	*Kree-ree*	Daughter of Ceridwen and Lord Tegid
Cymru	*Cuhm-ree*	Wales
Dinas Affaraon	*Deen-as Aff-ar-ay-on*	Otherworldly abode of the Druid Alchemists
Dinas Emrys	*Deen-as Em-riss*	Another name for Dinas Affaraon
Elphin	*Elfin*	Fisherman who fostered Gwion
Eryri	*Eh-ruh-ree*	Snowdonia, the National Park
Fferyllt	*Fair-eellt*	Legendary druid alchemists
Gwion	*Gwee-on*	Taliesin before his transformation
Lloegr	*Hll-oy-ger*	England

Llyn	*Hll-in*	A lake
Llyn Tegid	*Hll-in-Tegid*	Lake Bala
Morfran	*Mor-vran*	Utter darkness (another name for Afagddu)
Môr Hafren	*Mor Hav-ren*	Bristol Channel
Taliesin	*Tal-yes-in*	The Great Bard
Ynys Enlli	*Uh-nis En-hlli*	Bardsey Island
Ynys Môn	*Uh-nis Mohn*	Isle of Anglesey
Yr Wyddfa	*Er-With-va*	Mount Snowdon, the highest mountain in Wales

References

Chapter One
Quoted from the book *The Mist-Filled Path*, Copyright © 2002 by
Frank MacEowen. Reprinted with permission by New World
Library, Novato, CA, www.newworldlibrary.com.

Chapter Two
"Singing Bowl" published in *Kindred Spirit Magazine* and
Heartsong, from a creative writing task set by Steve Hitchins,
Workers Educational Association, Wales.

Chapter Five
Helen Raphael Sands, *Labyrinth: Pathway to Meditation and
Healing*, Gaia Books London 2002.
Lauren Artress, *Walking a Sacred Path*, Berkley Publishing 1995.
Quoted from Philip Carr-Gomm in the book *Sacred Places*, p. 96,
Quercus 2008.

Chapter Seven
Meditation Walk, Canyon Ranch, Arizona, early 1990s.

Chapter Nine
Quoted from Matthew Fox, *The Coming of the Cosmic Christ*, p. 58,
HarperOne (Harper Collins) 1988.
Ritual and Meditation workshop with Penny Billington and
Matt McCabe in association with The Order of Bards, Ovates
and Druids.

Chapter Twelve
Hallowquest: Tarot Magic and the Arthurian Mysteries, also *The
Arthurian Tarot* pack, John and Caitlin Mathews, Aquarian
Press 1990.

The Medicine Cards, Jamie Sams and David Carson, illustrated by Angela C. Werneke, Bear and Co. 1998.

The Order of Bards, Ovates and Druids teachings on ritual and seasonal celebrations.

Chapter Fourteen

The search for Taliesin's legend and the Snowdonia trip were inspired by a Bardic Grade correspondence course with The Order of Bards, Ovates and Druids, https://druidry.org.

Chapter Fifteen

The Black Book of Carmarthen, Anonymous, Myth Bank 2020, also in the National Library of Wales Archives.

Walesonline.com.

Chapter Sixteen

The Lord of the Rings, The Fellowship of the Ring, J.R.R. Tolkien.

The Secret Garden, Frances Hodgson-Burnett.

Chalice Well Guidebook and *Chalice Well Essences,* Chalice Well Trust, www.chalicewell.org.uk.

Chapter Seventeen

Quotation from Alice O. Howell, *The Dove in the Stone,* p. 93, Quest Books 1988.

Syon, Syon Park Ltd. 2003.

Chapter Eighteen

Quoted from *Siddhartha,* Hermann Hesse, 1922, p. 123, Macmillan Collector's Library edition 2020.

Second editions of poems by Iona Jenkins.

"Grail Quest," original version with the title of "Grail" in *The Starlit Door,* 2017.

"The Language of Angels," original version in *Heartsong,* 2016.

Suggested Further Reading and Resources

A Handbook of Angels, H.C. Moolenburgh, C.W. Daniel 1984.

Heartsong: A Collection of Poetry and Reflections, Iona Jenkins 2016, www.ionajenkins.com.

The Starlit Door, Poetry and Reflections, Iona Jenkins 2017, www.ionajenkins.com.

The Path of Druidry: Walking the Ancient Green Way, Penny Billington, Llewellen 2011.

The Druid Mysteries: Ancient Wisdom for the 21st Century, Philip Carr-Gomm, Random House 2002.

The Miracle of Mindfulness, Thich Nhat Hanh, Rider/Random House 1991.

The Art of Living, His Holiness the Dalai Lama, Thorsons 2001.

Christ of the Celts: The Healing of Creation, J. Philip Newell, Jossey-Bass 2007.

The Coming of the Cosmic Christ, Matthew Fox, HarperOne (Harper Collins) 1988.

The Circle of Life: The Heart's Journey Through the Seasons, Joyce Rupp and Macrina Wiederkehr, Sorin Books 2005.

The Dove in the Stone: Finding the Sacred in the Commonplace, Alice O. Howell, Quest Books 1988.

The Hidden Life of Trees, Peter Wohlleben, William Collins 2017.

The Arthurian Tarot, John and Caitlin Mathews, Aquarian Press 1990.

Hallowquest: Tarot Magic and the Arthurian Mysteries, John and Caitlin Mathews, Aquarian Press 1990.

The Creative Connection: Expressive Arts as Healing, Natalie Rogers, PCCS Books 1993.

Walking a Sacred Path: Rediscovering the Labyrinth as a Spiritual Practice, Lauren Artress, Berkley Publishing 1995.

Labyrinth: Pathway to Meditation and Healing, Helen Raphael Sands, Gaia Books London 2000.

The Mist-Filled Path, Frank MacEowen, New World Library 2002.

Yearning for the Wind, Tom Cowan, New World Library 2003.

Sacred Places: Sites of Spiritual Pilgrimage from Stonehenge to Santiago De Compostela, Philip Carr-Gomm, Quercus 2008, 2011.

What We Ache For: Creativity and the Unfolding of Your Soul, Oriah Mountain Dreamer, Harper Collins 2005.

Rumi: Selected Poems, Penguin Books 1999, and reissued under present title in 2004.

Kindling the Celtic Spirit, Mara Freeman, HarperOne (Harper Collins) 2001.

The Artist's Way, Julia Cameron 1993, republished by Macmillan 2016.

Why the moon travels, Oein DeBhairduin, Skein Press 2020, is an inspiring book of tales, beautifully written by the author in Irish Traveller tradition.

The Druid Animal Oracle Deck, Philip and Stephanie Carr-Gomm. Illustrated by Bill Worthington. Connection Book Publishing 2005.

The Medicine Cards: The Discovery of Power Through the Ways of Animals, Jamie Sams and David Carson. Illustrated by Angela C. Werneke. Bear and Co. 1988.

Rumi Oracle: An Invitation to the Heart of the Divine, Alana Fairchild. Artwork and translation by Rassouli. Blue Angel Publishing 2016.

Siddhartha, Hermann Hesse, Macmillan Collector's Library 2020 (first published in 1922).

The Lord of the Rings, J.R.R. Tolkien, Harper Collins 2020.

The Order of Bards, Ovates and Druids, https://druidry.org.

The Chalice Well, The Chalice Well Trust, www.chalicewell.org.uk.

Syon Park, Syon Park Ltd., www.syonpark.co.uk.

The Royal Botanic Gardens Kew, www.kew.org.

Snowdon Mountain Railway, info https://Snowdonrailway. co.uk.

)HN HUNT PUBLISHIN(

O-BOOKS

SPIRITUALITY

O is a symbol of the world, of oneness and unity; this eye represents knowledge and insight. We publish titles on general spirituality and living a spiritual life. We aim to inform and help you on your own journey in this life.

If you have enjoyed this book, why not tell other readers by posting a review on your preferred book site?

Recent bestsellers from O-Books are:

Heart of Tantric Sex

Diana Richardson

Revealing Eastern secrets of deep love and intimacy to Western couples.

Paperback: 978-1-90381-637-0 ebook: 978-1-84694-637-0

Crystal Prescriptions

The A-Z guide to over 1,200 symptoms and their healing crystals

Judy Hall

The first in the popular series of eight books, this handy little guide is packed as tight as a pill-bottle with crystal remedies for ailments.

Paperback: 978-1-90504-740-6 ebook: 978-1-84694-629-5

Take Me To Truth
Undoing the Ego
Nouk Sanchez, Tomas Vieira
The best-selling step-by-step book on shedding the Ego, using the teachings of *A Course In Miracles*.
Paperback: 978-1-84694-050-7 ebook: 978-1-84694-654-7

The 7 Myths about Love...Actually!
The Journey from your HEAD to the HEART of your SOUL
Mike George
Smashes all the myths about LOVE.
Paperback: 978-1-84694-288-4 ebook: 978-1-84694-682-0

The Holy Spirit's Interpretation of the New Testament
A Course in Understanding and Acceptance
Regina Dawn Akers
Following on from the strength of *A Course In Miracles*, NTI teaches us how to experience the love and oneness of God.
Paperback: 978-1-84694-085-9 ebook: 978-1-78099-083-5

The Message of A Course In Miracles
A translation of the Text in plain language
Elizabeth A. Cronkhite
A translation of *A Course in Miracles* into plain, everyday language for anyone seeking inner peace. The companion volume, *Practicing A Course In Miracles*, offers practical lessons and mentoring.
Paperback: 978-1-84694-319-5 ebook: 978-1-84694-642-4

Your Simple Path
Find Happiness in every step
Ian Tucker
A guide to helping us reconnect with what is really important in our lives.
Paperback: 978-1-78279-349-6 ebook: 978-1-78279-348-9

365 Days of Wisdom
Daily Messages To Inspire You Through The Year
Dadi Janki
Daily messages which cool the mind, warm the heart and guide you along your journey.
Paperback: 978-1-84694-863-3 ebook: 978-1-84694-864-0

Body of Wisdom
Women's Spiritual Power and How it Serves
Hilary Hart
Bringing together the dreams and experiences of women across the world with today's most visionary spiritual teachers.
Paperback: 978-1-78099-696-7 ebook: 978-1-78099-695-0

Dying to Be Free
From Enforced Secrecy to Near Death to True Transformation
Hannah Robinson
After an unexpected accident and near-death experience, Hannah Robinson found herself radically transforming her life, while a remarkable new insight altered her relationship with her father, a practising Catholic priest.
Paperback: 978-1-78535-254-6 ebook: 978-1-78535-255-3

The Ecology of the Soul
A Manual of Peace, Power and Personal Growth for Real People
in the Real World
Aidan Walker
Balance your own inner Ecology of the Soul to regain your
natural state of peace, power and wellbeing.
Paperback: 978-1-78279-850-7 ebook: 978-1-78279-849-1

Not I, Not other than I
The Life and Teachings of Russel Williams
Steve Taylor, Russel Williams
The miraculous life and inspiring teachings of one of the World's
greatest living Sages.
Paperback: 978-1-78279-729-6 ebook: 978-1-78279-728-9

On the Other Side of Love
A woman's unconventional journey towards wisdom
Muriel Maufroy
When life has lost all meaning, what do you do?
Paperback: 978-1-78535-281-2 ebook: 978-1-78535-282-9

Practicing A Course In Miracles
A translation of the Workbook in plain language, with
mentor's notes
Elizabeth A. Cronkhite
The practical second and third volumes of The Plain-Language
A Course In Miracles.
Paperback: 978-1-84694-403-1 ebook: 978-1-78099-072-9

Quantum Bliss
The Quantum Mechanics of Happiness, Abundance, and Health
George S. Mentz
Quantum Bliss is the breakthrough summary of success and
spirituality secrets that customers have been waiting for.
Paperback: 978-1-78535-203-4 ebook: 978-1-78535-204-1

The Upside Down Mountain
Mags MacKean
A must-read for anyone weary of chasing success and happiness
– one woman's inspirational journey swapping the uphill slog for
the downhill slope.
Paperback: 978-1-78535-171-6 ebook: 978-1-78535-172-3

Your Personal Tuning Fork
The Endocrine System
Deborah Bates
Discover your body's health secret, the endocrine system, and
'twang' your way to sustainable health!
Paperback: 978-1-84694-503-8 ebook: 978-1-78099-697-4

Readers of ebooks can buy or view any of these bestsellers by
clicking on the live link in the title. Most titles are published
in paperback and as an ebook. Paperbacks are available in
traditional bookshops. Both print and ebook formats are
available online.
Find more titles and sign up to our readers' newsletter at
http://www.johnhuntpublishing.com/mind-body-spirit
Follow us on Facebook at https://www.facebook.com/OBooks/
and Twitter at https://twitter.com/obooks